HOW TO WRITE A BESTSELLING SELF-HELP BOOK

The 68 Fatal Mistakes You Should Avoid

JEAN MARIE STINE

PageTurner Editions

ISBN 978-1500791278
All rights reserved
Copyright © 2002, 2012, 2014 Jean Marie Stine
This book may not be reproduced in whole or in part without written permission.
For information contact:
PageTurnerEditions.com
A Renaissance E Books publication

DEDICATION

To Self-Help/How-To
Writers Everywhere

May your dreams become
books
And may your books fulfill
your dreams

CONTENTS

Introduction   i

PART ONE: MISTAKES IN YOUR PROPOSAL   1
Mistake #1 – Failure to Make It a Sales Document
Mistake #2 – Failure to Include Key Elements in Your Book Proposal
Mistake #3 – Not Including Adequate "About This Book" Section
Mistake #4 – Not Including Adequate "About Marketing" Section
Mistake #5 – Not Including Adequate "About Publicity" Section
Mistake #6 – Not Including Adequate "About Production" Section
Mistake #7 – Not Including Adequate "About the Author" Section
Mistake #8 – Not Including Adequate "About Supportive Material" Section
Mistake #9 – Failure to Include Adequate Writing Sample

PART TWO: MISTAKES IN YOUR PREFACE   21
Mistake #10 – Failure to Include Key Elements of a Preface
Mistake #11 – Not Establishing Who Book is For
Mistake #12 – Not Establishing Your Credentials
Mistake #13 – Not Explaining Why You Wrote the Book
Mistake #14 – Not Establishing Success of Your Program or System

Mistake #15 – Not Alerting Readers to Anything Special about Your Overall Approach
Mistake #16 – Failure to Include Brief Overview of Book

PART THREE: MISTAKES IN WRITING CHAPTERS   33

Mistake #18 – Failure to Make Chapter Titles Understandable and Interesting
Mistake #19 – Not Painting a Picture of the Book in Chapter One
Mistake #20 – Lack of Introductory Overview Paragraph in Every Chapter
Mistake #21 – Not Linking Chapter to Book's Theme and Previous Chapters
Mistake #22 – Not Sticking to a Strong Chapter Structure
Mistake #23 – Not Getting to the Subject of a Chapter Immediately
Mistake #24 – Infrequent Use of Headings and Subheadings
Mistake #25 – Failure to Introduce Each Section Within a Chapter
Mistake #26 – Failure to Use Bulleted Lists
Mistake #27 – Failure to Bring Each Chapter to a Formal Conclusion
Mistake #28 – Making Chapters Too Long or Too Short

PART FOUR: MISTAKES IN WRITING & STYLE   52

Mistake #29 – Failure to Write in an Everyday, Easy-to-Understand Style

Mistake #30 – Lack of Topic Sentences
Mistake #31 – Using the Wrong Word Instead of the Right One
Mistake #32 – Using Vague Pronouns that Could Refer to Anything
Mistake #33 – Use of Overly Abstract Language
Mistake #34 – Failure to Rein-In Run-On Sentences
Mistake #35 – Using Overly Wordy Writing
Mistake #36 – Failure to Define Professional, Trade and Technical Terms
Mistake #37 – Using Negative Comparisons
Mistake #38 – Failure to Write the Reader into the Book
Mistake #39 – Writing More about Yourself than the Reader

PART FIVE: PRESENTING STEPS OR ELEMENTS OF YOUR PROGRAM   73
Mistake #40 – Inconsistent Formatting
Mistake #41 – Failure to Explicitly State the Problem at the Beginning
Mistake #42 – Using the Same Opening "Hook" Every Time
Mistake #43 – Not Using a New Heading to Highlight Each New Step of Your Program or Exercise
Mistake #44 – Not Creating Unique Formatting that Captures Reader Imagination
Mistake #45 – Failure to Make Instructions Direct and To the Point
Mistake #46 – Not Fully Explaining Exercises Before Presenting Them
Mistake #47 – Not Spelling Out Exercises in Numbered Steps

Mistake #48 – Not Illustrating How Each Step Works
Mistake #49 – Making Exercises Overly Lengthy or Complicated
Mistake #50 – Failure to Sum Up Exercises

PART SIX: MISTAKES IN USING QUOTATIONS & CASE HISTORIES   92
Mistake #51 – Over- or Under-relying on Quotes from Other Authorities
Mistake #52 – Not Highlighting the Points of Quotations
Mistake #53 – Failure to Illustrate Points with Anecdotes or Case Histories
Mistake #54 – Inconsistency in Anecdote Formatting
Mistake #55 – Using Transcripts Rather than Case Histories
Mistake #56 – Not Making the People in Your Case Histories Come Alive

PART SEVEN: OTHER CRITICAL MISTAKES   104
Mistake #57 – Failure to Fully Develop Important Ideas and Concepts
Mistake #58 – Not Supplying Concrete Examples
Mistake #59 – Failing to Double-Check All Facts
Mistake #60 – Overloading the Book with Too Many Subjects and Goals
Mistake #61 – Failing to Answer Questions Raised in Your Book
Mistake #62 – Trying to Solve Your Writing Problems On Your Own
Mistake #63 – Relying on Repetition, Redundancy and Pet Phrases
Mistake #64 – Not Fully Identifying Famous People

Cited in the Text
Mistake #65 – Failure to Coin Exciting Buzzwords that Grab Reader Attention

CONCLUSION: THE THREE WORST MISTAKES AFTER PUBLICATION   126
Mistake #66 – Blaming the Publisher if Your Book Doesn't Sell
Mistake #67 – Giving Up on Your Book
Mistake #68 – Not Writing Another Book

APPENDICES   133
A: One Chapter and a Short Description – All You Need to Sell Your Book
B: The Self-Help Writer's Manuscript Review Checklist

Recommended Reading   143

INTRODUCTION

"Publishers today only want books that don't need editing."
Pat Teal, literary agent

"Mergers and consolidations in the publishing industry have meant staff cutbacks and a stronger orientation on marketing the books that are published, with the result that there are fewer editors and those few must devote more time to sales and promotional details. As a result, most editors no longer have time to edit."
Publisher's Weekly

This book has been written with all those in mind who want to write self-help/how-to books in fields like personal growth, business, sports, recovery, health, New Age, spirituality, hobbies and crafts. It is intended as a guide for:

* Psychologists, psychiatrists and other mental health professionals
* Physicians, nurses and physical therapists
* Facilitators, therapists and counselors
* Athletes, coaches and other sports professionals
* CEOs, managers and team leaders
* Tarot readers, astrologers and psychics
* Ministers, rabbis and other members of the clergy
* Artisans, artists and other craftspeople
* Hobbyists, collectors and antiquarians

If you fit in one of the above categories – or have any other form of expertise and want to share that know-how with others – then this book is for you.

Once upon a time, a writer like Thomas Wolfe, John Updike or Samuel Delaney with a brilliant – but flawed – manuscript, could count on visionary publishers and editors to see their book's potential and work with them to perfect the work. Today, editors have less and less time to edit and are increasingly reluctant to take on manuscripts that require extensive work. That makes it harder for beginning writers, who naturally make more mistakes, to sell their manuscripts.

That may seem to weight the odds against novice writers. As an aspiring self-help author who is an expert in your subject but a novice at writing, how can you possibly be expected to submit a manuscript so well-polished that it doesn't need editing? And, of course, your book can't become a bestseller unless a publisher accepts it.

Don't despair! There is an answer. You can do what seasoned, professional self-help/how-to writers do – learn to troubleshoot your own book, eliminating potential defects before you expose your manuscript to the critical eyes of publishers, editors or agents.

During my years as a self-help/how-to editor, I saw thousands of self-help manuscripts rejected because of the same oft-repeated, common mistakes. It is my hope to save you from making those mistakes, to show you how to identify them yourself and avoid them. Then you can submit your manuscript with confidence, knowing it is free of the errors that cause ninety-nine out of a hundred manuscripts to go unpublished.

Before starting this book, I carefully reviewed stacks of rejected self-help manuscripts from aspiring authors. I also looked at first drafts which publishers had asked me to rewrite before they were deemed suitable for publication. I kept a running list of the defects I noted. Altogether, I found 69 key mistakes most inexperienced authors seemed to make.

These 69 mistakes include:

*Not including the Seven Key Elements in your book proposal
*Not including the Seven Key Elements of a good preface
*Not using the first chapter to paint a picture of your entire book
*Failing to link each chapter to the book's theme, and to previous chapters
*Neglecting to stick to a strong, focused chapter structure
*Infrequent use of headings
*Neglecting to use bulleted lists
*Failure to write in an everyday, easy-to-understand style
*Using negative comparisons
*Not remembering to define technical or special words
*Failing to write the reader into the book
*Not making instructions direct and to the point
*Failure to fully explain exercises before presenting them

In this book I describe each of the 69 key mistakes so that you can recognize them when you see them in your own work. Then I explain how you can avoid or correct the problem. The result should be a zero-defect manuscript and book proposal that will sail through the editorial and publishing committees to acceptance.

I've taught multiple writing workshops, and I've seen the difference this approach makes in revising messy first manuscripts. Will it help your book? I'll let some of the first-time authors I've worked with answer that question. Here's what they have to say:

"After just one session with Jean, I sold my first book for $35,000." John Holmstron, author of *Answered Prayers*.

"After Jean showed me how to revise my manuscript, the paperback edition of my book went for $127,500." Timmen Cermak, Ph.D., author of *A Time to Heal*.

"If you follow only a third of her advice, you'll have a successful book." Jeremy Tarcher, publisher, Putnam Books.

This book is divided into seven parts, one for each of the key areas of self-help/how-to writing. Part One focuses on common mistakes in writing Proposals. Part Two looks at mistakes in writing Prefaces. Part Three describes mistakes most often made in writing chapters. Part Four covers errors in writing and style. Part Five, errors in using quotations from other sources, as well as those involving anecdotes or case histories. Part Six details deadly errors in presenting the elements of your program and exercises. Part Seven points out mistakes like failing to double-check facts, failing to answer all the questions you raise in your book, repetition, and more. One appendix explains how you can sell your self-help book to publishers with just two chapters and a Proposal. The second appendix provides a checklist you can use to troubleshoot your manuscript for key errors after you complete your first draft.

This book has been designed to be the only book on self-help writing you will ever need. In the course of showing you what not to do, it also teaches you what to do. When you finish, you will know everything you need to know to write a self-help or how-to book with "bestseller" written all over it.

Jean Marie Stine

PART ONE

MISTAKES IN YOUR PROPOSAL

Your book will never become a million-copy bestseller if you can't sell it to a publisher. What follows are the most common weaknesses in book proposals that cause publishers to reject them.

MISTAKE #1
Failure to Make Your Proposal a Sales Document

Many novice writers are overly modest about describing their book and themselves as its author. The Proposal is a sales document, somewhere in style between a publisher's advertisement for a book and a prospectus for a small business. Its only purpose is to convince a publisher to contract for your book. If you can't make your book sound exciting, with strong sales potential, it is doomed to fail even before you mail it off.

I know it can be hard sometimes to "toot your own horn." Beginners hesitate to over-praise their work, or to use the kind of bold adjectives found in book advertisements and publisher's catalogues. They shy away from words like "breakthrough," "extraordinary," "insightful," "unique," "illuminating," "compelling." But think about it for a moment. If publishers think these are hot buzzwords that will excite readers, then it stands to reason that these are hot buzzwords that excite publishers as well.

Hint: If getting your book published is a priority, begin by going online and reading publisher's descriptions of books like yours. Incorporate the kind of words and phrases you find there into your own Proposal.

MISTAKE #2
Failure to Include Key Elements

As a document designed to convince editors and publishers to buy your book, your Proposal will fail miserably unless it includes certain vital sections. Each of these sections helps build the case that yours is a book worth publishing and you are the person to write it. Omit one, and you may be leaving out the keystone element that would have sold your book.

Here are the key elements you should include in the Proposal for your book:

1. About This Book
   Overview
   Comparison with Competition
   Important Questions This Book will Answer
   Important Skills the Reader Will Learn
2. About Marketing
   Audience
   Sales
3. Publicity
   Book Reviews
   Author Interviews
4. About Production
   Estimated Length
   Estimated Time of Completion
   Illustrative Material
   Special Features

5. About the Author
   Biography
   Vita
   Other Books
   Publications
   Newspaper and Magazines Where Author has been Profiled
   Electronic Media Where Author has been Featured
   Lectures, Workshops, Speeches
6. Supportive Material
   Articles about Author
   Articles by Author
   Announcements of Classes and Speaking Engagements
   Endorsements
7. Writing Sample
   Chapter Outline
   Introduction
   Sample Chapter

MISTAKE #3
Inadequate "About This Book" Section

This is the most important part of your Proposal in many ways. It is where potential editors and publishers will start. You want to explain as clearly as possible why people will want your book, what makes it unique, and that there is a significant readership that will benefit from and buy it. Complete this section correctly and you will have publishers salivating to read your sample material.

The About This Book section should contain a sub-section titled "Overview," which should give a one to two page description of your book that covers:

1. What the book is about
2. Who will want to read it
3. How readers will benefit from reading your book

Following the Overview should be a "Comparison and Competition" page, briefly covering the top six to ten books that offer yours competition or address the same subject. In a paragraph each, explain each book's approach to the subject and what makes your approach new or special – what it offers the reader that those books do not. This is key research that you should be doing for yourself anyways, and it is something that publishers care about passionately.

Finally, your About This Book section should conclude with a series of lists (no more than a page each) that allow editorial and marketing people to quickly reference the key elements of your book. This is where you place your buzzwords. These lists should include, "Important Questions This Book will Answer," "Important Skills/Benefits the Reader Will Learn," plus any others you consider relevant.

MISTAKE #4
Inadequate "About Marketing" Section

Novice writers skimp here too. They assume the publisher will know how to sell their book. And if your book is on "13 Ways to Rekindle Your Romance," this may indeed be true. But if it is more specialized – golf, inspirational, recovery, model trains – you may know of avenues for sales, like specialty catalogues or stores, that a general publisher couldn't possibly be aware of. Spending time on this helps to build your case that there is indeed a market for your book. If you leave it up to chance, you may cause your book to miss out on vital sales that could make the difference between its success and failure.

The second section of your Proposal (following "About this Book") should be given a heading like "About Marketing." It should explain who would purchase your book and how to sell it.

The first subsection should be titled "Audience" and detail the book's potential readership. Give any statistics on the size of the audience you can come up with. Hint: Most books have more than one potential audience. For instance, a book on basic golfing techniques might be aimed at novice golfers. But it might also benefit seasoned players who want to brush up their game. It might also be of interest to golfing instructors who are looking for an easy way to teach beginners. That's three potential readerships, not one! Or if your book is about recovering from childhood abuse, it might appeal to:

  1. Those abused as children
  2. Professionals treating them
  3. Family and loved ones seeking to understand them

This should be followed by a section on "Sales" which lists all your ideas for how your book could be sold and marketed. "General bookstores" may seem like a no-brainer. But some books are so specialized they wouldn't be of interest to the general public and would be better off being sold in specialty stores like pet stores, health food stores and sporting goods emporiums.

So, if your book does appeal to the general public, head your list with "General Bookstores."

If there are specialty stores in your area of expertise that might also carry it, list them next; for instance, "Health food stores."

What about catalogues? Are there any specialty mail-order catalogues that your book might be a good fit for? If so, list them; for instance, "The Complete Golfer's Catalogue" and "Golf-o-Rama."

Are there any organizations that might want to sell it to their members? Crafters and hobbyists often have organizations that provide a built-in audience for a book. Would your book be purchased by companies in order to run workshops for their managers? Are there professional groups or guilds that would find your book relevant?

Perhaps "Recovery Groups" if your book is on recovery.

Is there a strong mail-order market? Many publishers have mail-order divisions to help maximize sales of their books. Mail-order works best when you can get a large list of names and addresses of people interested in the subject of your book. If you were writing about skiing, for example, you could go to skiing organizations and publications. Likely they would sell you or your publisher their lists of members and subscribers. If "Mail-order" is a strong marketing venue for your book, put in a heading for that, and list places where the appropriate lists can be obtained.

What about coupon advertising in specialty publications? If you are writing, say, about how to build model trains, you probably know of magazines for model train enthusiasts. People who read them might well order your book if they saw a tasteful ad with a coupon below which they could easily fill out and mail in. Add "Coupon advertising" to your list, and cite the publications where you believe coupon ads should be placed.

And what about college courses? A book on "How to Grow Your Business" might well be the perfect text for classes and seminars in operating a small or beginning business. If you can think of any academic use for your book, add "Course adoptions" to your Marketing list, and cite the kinds of classes you think would be a good fit.

Don't forget libraries! Nothing goes without saying when it comes to helping convincing a publisher to publish your book. If you think it is a book that libraries will want, add "Libraries" to your list and say why it will be needed by their patrons.

MISTAKE #5
Inadequate "About Publicity" Section

Publicity, not advertising, is what sells books. Reviews and author interviews are what inspire readers to go forth in search of a specific book. Here again, the author may often know of local or specialty media willing to review her or his book that the publisher would be unaware of. Failure to include these outlets may convince the publisher that there aren't enough venues to generate adequate publicity, resulting in a rejection of the entire book proposal.

This section should cover any possible sources of free publicity you think might be interested in your book. It should be divided into two parts: "Book Reviews" and "Author Interviews."

Under "Book Reviews" include every publication you can think of that might be interested in your book. If you are writing about a topic of interest to a small, but devoted audience, like model airplane building, it isn't likely the *New York Times* or *Newsweek* will review your book. On the other hand, if you are writing about recovery from alcoholism, self-esteem, business, rekindling romantic intimacy, or athletics, there is a good chance there may be some national publications that are interested in reviewing your book. If so, list them and explain why you think your book will be of appeal to their editors and readers.

If there are specialty magazines, like fitness, recovery, athletic, or women's publications in the subject area of your book, list each magazine title, and again explain why you think your book will be of appeal to their editors and readers.

Divide your Author Interviews list into two parts: "Print Media" and "Electronic Media."

Under Print Media, jot down every publication you think might be interested in doing an article on you and your book, along with why. Include:

1. National publications
2. Regional publications
3. Specialty publications

Again, follow the same sensible guidelines given above about Book Reviews. Be ambitious but reasonable in thinking about potential sources of publicity. Be sure to give strong reasons for why a publication would be interested in talking to you. Hint: Don't overlook your local magazines and newspapers. They love to feature interviews about local people who have done something notable – like writing a book.

Beneath the heading of Electronic Media, first list any national, local or specialty television programs that in the past have featured books like yours. Then do the same for national, local or specialty radio shows.

MISTAKE #6
Inadequate "About Production" Section

Not getting this section right won't cause your book to be rejected. But it will lead to confusion and cost overruns for the publisher in the long run – and you won't be too popular with your publisher after that.

This section focuses on anything that affects the production of your book. The "About Production" material should include the likely length of your book, how long it will take for you to write it, and whether there will be illustrative or other special material.

Under the heading "Estimated Length," type the approximate number of manuscript pages or words you believe your book will be. Publishers need to know so they can estimate what to charge readers for your book. Obviously longer books cost more to produce and must sell for more, and vice versa.

Publishers also need to know the "Estimated Time of Completion" for your manuscript (also known as the Delivery Date). Will it take you six months, a year, eighteen months? Knowing this helps them work out their publication schedule.

Next comes "Illustrative Material." The use of photographs, charts, and line illustrations (like cartoons) adds to the cost of producing your book. Again, the publisher needs to know whether your book will include these, in order to estimate publication cost and bookstore price.

Finally, "Special Features." Here you list any other elements you would like to include that might affect the production, and therefore, cost of your book – tables, chronologies, and so forth. For example, you might wish to include ten blank horoscope charts in a book on do-it-yourself astrology.

MISTAKE #7
Inadequate "About the Author" Section

Don't be shy. That's fatal for your book. This is where you sell the publisher on the fact that you are highly qualified to write your book. Hold back here due to modesty or the feeling that you might be perceived as bragging, and you probably blow your chances of having your book accepted for publication! Tooting your own horn and boasting about your accomplishments and background are the order of the day.

The fourth section of your Proposal is all about you. Without offending anyone, I'd like to say that metaphorically, your job here is to make yourself sound like the literary equivalent of the Second Coming of Christ. Where they are applicable to your own life, your "About the Author" section should feature:

A 250-500 word "Biography" of yourself that should focus entirely on the aspects of your life that contribute to your being qualified to write your book. This is where you establish yourself as an expert, as the one person supremely qualified to bring this book to fruition. Your domestic arrangements, hobbies, pets, and any other activities not related to the book can be left out. You will be asked for them later, if your book is selected for publication.

This should be followed by a list of your

educational and professional experience, aka your "Vita."

If you have written any "Other Books," be sure to list them under that heading.

If you have written articles for professional publications, local or specialty magazines, or even the *New York Times*, then list them all. Each entry helps build the case that you know your beans about writing.

Next, if you have ever been interviewed by any print publication of any kind, list it under "Newspaper and Magazines Where Author has been Profiled." If you have been interviewed, this notifies publishers that you are an experienced interview subject. It gives them confidence that you can handle publicity appearances, and that there is already a potential audience for your book in the form of the people who have read those interviews.

Jot down any "Electronic Media Where Author has been Featured." If you have ever done a local, specialty or national television or radio interview, publishers will eat you up with a spoon. Radio and television reach far bigger audiences than magazines and newspapers and each such appearance by you means you have already generated a large potential readership.

If you know your subject inside and out, it is likely that at some point you will have delivered "Lectures, Workshops, and Speeches" on it or other topics. List them all – wherever, whenever and whatever. Each adds further support to the case for your:

* Expertise on your subject
* Ability to publicize your book in interviews
* Preexisting audience of those who have heard you speak, lecture, teach

MISTAKE #8
Inadequate "About Supportive Material" Section

You want to close out the "sales" portion of your Proposal with a section titled "About Supportive Material." The idea is to include in your Proposal photocopies of additional documentation supporting your expertise and celebrity – from articles about you to endorsements for your ideas or program. List each major category you have material for (see below) in the Proposal, and include the documents themselves when you mail it in to an agent or publisher.

The rule here is: If you've got it, flaunt it. This is another area where holding back due to modesty will only hurt your book's chances of being accepted by a publisher. This is "show and tell" time, and the more visual aids showing that you have the credentials to write your book, the better. Leave them out, and you may be leaving the clincher out of your sales pitch.

Start with any "Articles about Author." Use photocopies of any publications mentioning you, from a one-sentence entry to an entire article.

Follow this with any "Articles by Author." If there are a large number, include several complete articles and the first pages of half a dozen more.

If they exist, include up to a dozen or more "Announcements of Classes and Speaking Engagements" you've had. These help reinforce the fact that you are an articulate, experienced speaker, with expertise.

Don't forget "Endorsements." If you have letters from other experts in your subject that help attest to the effectiveness of your ideas, or from those who have tried them and discovered how well they work, include all you can. Ditto letters from any radio or television shows you have appeared on that are reflective of the same theme.

Include a photo of yourself. The publisher will want to know how you will look on the back of your book's jacket and on television.

MISTAKE #9
Inadequate Writing Sample

Don't stint on your "Writing Sample." After all, it is what shows you have an exciting, informative book, plus the ability and know-how to write it.

This section should include your outline for the book as well as one or more sample chapters. Your "Chapter Outline" should not just list the titles of your chapters. Instead, add in a word or short phrase to show the key ideas to be covered within each chapter.

Most experienced authors usually include the Preface to their book and one to three "Sample Chapters," depending on their length. Aim for a total of around 50 pages, or slightly more, of material.

PART TWO
MISTAKES IN YOUR PREFACE

Whether you call it your "Preface" or "Introduction" or "Foreword" isn't important. What's important is that it's the first part of your book many readers encounter. And we all know how important first impressions are. If mistakes cost you readers here, you can wave good-by to bestsellerdom.

MISTAKE #10
Failure to Include the Key Elements of a Preface

The Preface is the place to provide any and all background material necessary to understand the book as a whole. Get it wrong, and you can almost guarantee you will lose a significant percentage of your readers. Get it right and every single reader will turn eagerly to Chapter One.

A well-constructed Preface includes:

* Who your book is for
* Your credentials (what qualifies you to write it)
* Why and/or how you came to write it
* Evidence your system is successful
* Anything special about the book or your overall approach
* Brief overview of parts and chapters
* Hopeful, upbeat conclusion

MISTAKE #11
Not Establishing Who Your Book is For

The very first thing any reader wants to know is whether a book is about them, whether it addresses their problems and interests. When readers don't see themselves in your pages immediately, they become restless and disconnected. They begin to "tune out" – even laying your book aside, intending to pick it up later – but more often, never getting back to it at all. That's why you want to begin with a one to three paragraph description of who your book is written for. If there is more than one group, be certain you mention them all. For example, your book could just be for people seeking to manage their anger. But it could also be written for the therapists who work with anger management, families and loved ones impacted by this issue, researchers, and anyone interested in understanding the roots of anger and possible transformative responses.

MISTAKE #12
Not Establishing Your Credentials

When you ask for advice, you generally want to hear from someone who knows what they're talking about. Readers will be more willing to follow your advice or program if they feel confident that it's coming from someone who has expertise. It doesn't so much matter to the reader whether that expertise is due to years of study and work as a professional, or from your own personal experience. Whether you've learned it or lived it, the reader will accept either path as qualifying you as an expert, able to write a book and dispense insights worth heeding. That's why you want to present your credentials as early in the book as possible – in the Preface. Having established your qualifications, you can be sure readers will read what follows with greater acceptance and attention.

MISTAKE #13
Not Explaining Why You Wrote the Book

There is a very important reason why you should tell the reader in the Preface about your own personal connection to your book: The Preface is your golden opportunity to make a personal connection with the reader right from the start. Everyone knows there's nothing like the personal touch. It's more often the personality of the saleswoman that makes the sale, rather than the product itself. And when someone in business takes the time to phone and apologize to you personally for a problem, don't you perk up – feel more comfortable with, and become more interested in them and their company? In the same way, when the reader experiences that immediate sense of connection with the author of a book, they feel they are in safe hands and begin to read with greater confidence and interest.

You can create that sense in your Preface by sharing the story of your own personal connection with your book. Whatever it was, take a few pages and tell the reader how you came to write the book. Was it a personal triumph over a difficult challenge? Was it something you noticed all your clients had in common during clinical practice? Was it the realization that all the books on how to play the game you coach are lacking a key element? Was it a series of events over the course of several years that led to a culminating insight? Seeing that you are a real person, with a personal interest in your work, will establish the all-important sense of connection that inspires readers to respond to what you write more deeply.

MISTAKE #14
Not Establishing the Success of Your Program or System

Another thing readers naturally want before investing their time and effort in your program is evidence that it will work for them. The world is full of people with systems, techniques, programs, insights and advice. Some are genuine and have something to offer, some are not and don't. Unless they get a sense that there is something to back up your program, they may relegate you to the latter category. Therefore it's critical that you present some evidence that what you are going to say is worth hearing. And, of course, to establish it before the reader begins Chapter One.

The evidence could be that your approach works for you and those you counseled. Or, it might be that you are an award-winning athlete who has taught your technique successfully to thousands. Or, it might be that by following certain principles, you built a neighborhood photocopying and print store into a thriving nationwide chain. Or, it might be that you are a psychologist who has performed clinical studies supporting the validity of your book.

This is the key selling point and indeed the key point of the Preface. Modesty must be set aside. Don't try to save any surprises for later. Instead, you need to give readers all the information they need about the success of your program. Only in this way will you convince them it's worth trying.

By the conclusion of your Preface, you should have so thoroughly established the efficacy of the system that no doubt remains in the reader's mind. They must be convinced they will receive beaucoups benefits from following it.

Remember: Don't say too little – or you may inadvertently undersell the reader on your book and your techniques.

MISTAKE #15
Not Alerting Readers to Anything Special About Your Overall Approach

The Preface is also the place to inform the reader of anything different about your overall approach to writing your book that they must know in order to understand it completely. If there is some aspect of your subject you have deliberately decided to omit (say, in a book on recovery from childhood sex abuse, focusing entirely on the victim and not discussing the psychology or motivations of the abuser) – say so in your Preface.

If you have written it with a deliberate bias, like the assumption that abortion is inherently right or wrong, let the reader know. Or if there is something they need to know in order to get the most from the book, like a specific approach to doing the exercises, place it in the Preface. Or it might be key background information, such as the fact that it was written just before the discovery that there is a genetic link to depression, and that the implications of the discovery will be dealt with in the Afterword.

If you fail to note these kinds of issues, the reader may misunderstand your book. They may become confused or irritated at a perceived but never explicitly stated bias – or even angry at a feeling of being misled. In almost every case, they will cease reading and not give your book the all important word-of-mouth that makes books bestsellers.

MISTAKE #16
Failure to Include a Brief Overview of the Book's Structure

Readers will peruse your Preface seeking some sense of what your book is about and what it will cover. They'll want to know if you are going to deal with the essential topics and issues connected with your subject. If they don't finish your Preface with a strong sense that your book covers this material, they will return it to the shelves unpurchased, or lay it aside never to return.

Instead, preview your book's main elements. Describe each chapter in a sentence or two. Give a clear sense of what your book covers, and perhaps what it does not. A person interested in advanced quilting techniques does not want to wade through a book of beginner patterns. Model train buffs may want to know if your book is focussed on HO scale or N scale trains. Giving a brief overview in the Preface of the material to be covered allows readers to make an informed choice. Confident that you deal with the subject thoroughly, they'll want to start Chapter One immediately.

MISTAKE #17
Failure to End on a Hopeful Note

If in your Preface you mention the problem on which your book focuses without mentioning that there is a solution, you will leave readers hanging. They may assume there is no help, that your book will just detail the problem – and they already know it exists. What they want to know is whether there is a remedy.

End your Preface on that note of hope by devoting a paragraph or so to the fact that there is indeed a solution. Offer readers a bit of description about what life promises if they follows your guidance. Readers will be eager to turn the page to Chapter One and begin learning how you can help them make their lives better.

Remember: The Preface is your ONE chance to convince readers you have something valuable to offer and that they should continue reading your book.

PART THREE
MISTAKES IN
WRITING CHAPTERS

The chapters are the heart of your book. If they are unfocused or disorganized, have boring titles, get off to a slow start or suffer from other critical defects, readers may have a hard time sticking with you. They may grow restless, begin thinking of other matters and soon abandon your book. You are asking readers for an investment of their time and attention. It is up to you to make it worth their while. The guidelines in this section will help you avoid common mistakes, helping to keep your readers engaged and enthusiastic.

MISTAKE #18
Failure to Make Chapter Titles Understandable and Interesting

Dreaming up good chapter titles takes a bit of effort – but there is a big payoff in terms of drawing readers into your book and helping them understand what it is all about. On the other hand, overly literal, academic, obscure, or trivializing chapter titles can turn readers off before they start reading. Remember, most books are still sold in bookstores, where most readers glance at a non-fiction book's table of contents to determine whether it seems interesting.

Literal titles like "The History of Iraq" lack warmth and excitement. Re-title the same material, "From Ancient Babylon to Modern Baghdad," and you lend the promise of colorful, engrossing material to your chapter title. Or combine the two versions for one that possesses both color and literalness: "From Ancient Babylon to Modern Baghdad: A Short History of Iraq." In short, don't call your first chapter, "What This Book Will Do." Instead call it, "Freedom from Nightmares at Last!"

Academic-sounding titles truly confer the kiss of death on a book, as far as reaching a wide audience of typical readers. Consider the title "An Anthropological Consideration of the Growth of Nicotine Addiction Among Women." Most readers will assume a book with weighty chapter titles like that is written only for academics and will look for another that seems written more on the level of the average person. On the other hand, a chapter title like "Women and Smoking: It's Getting to Be a Habit," sounds a lot more enticing and accessible.

Obscure chapter titles are another no-no. For instance, in a book on bullying, what would the chapter title "The Understanding" convey to you? Can you tell what the subject of the chapter will be? Probably not. But what if it was titled "The Intimidating Power of Fear: The Secret Understanding?" Might you then guess that part of the bullying phenomenon rested on one or both parties understanding the intimidating power of fear?

Using overly cute titles when writing about serious issues can give readers the impression your work is lightweight or trivial. For example, in a serious book about battered women, a chapter title like "Love May Be Blind, but Self-Preservation Keeps its Eyes Wide Open" might convey the idea that the book was a glib, superficial work. Something more along the lines of "Self-defense in Advance: The Six Signs of a Batterer" could suit your book better.

What makes a good chapter title? In essence, it is an exciting phrase that encapsulates in an interesting way the theme of your chapter.

To generate a good chapter title, first write down the subject. Next, look for well-known phrases that are related to or sound like it. Use them to make playful, hopeful or dramatic phrases that encapsulate the subject of your chapter. A title like "A Weighty Subject" for a chapter on obesity, for instance. Or an exciting promise, like "Putting Made Easy" for a book on golf. Or dramatic wording, like "Playing Beyond Your Limits" for a book on tennis.

Then use the checklist below to troubleshoot your titles like a professional. It is adapted from my paperback book, *Writing Successful How-To/Self-Help Books*.

Score one point for every "yes" you can give to the following questions about any prospective title you devise.

* Is it specific? (Does it say, "Make Money From Home" when you mean "In The Home Mail-order Business"?)

* Is your title arresting – attention-getting? (Does it say something flat and boring like, "The Encyclopedia of Sex," or catchy and exciting, like "Everything You Wanted to Know About Sex"?)

* Is it upbeat and positive? (Does it dwell on the negative or neutral, like "Being Lonely and Ignored," or does it emphasize the positive, like "Winning Friends and Influencing People"?)

* Does it offer the reader benefits? (Does it simply say "A Financial Guide to the Coming Recession," instead of promising to teach them "How to Make $1,000,000 per Year"?)

* Will readers know what you you're talking about? (Does it capture the problem in obscure terms like "Codependency and Intimacy: A Female Perspective" or in language anyone could recognize like "Women Who Love Too Much"?)

* Is it short? (Will it be easy to say? Most successful titles have less than six or seven words and are easy to remember.)

Total up the scores for each title. You should probably discard any title that only earned three points or less. Pick the one that has the highest score. Use it as your title. Hint: Save the rest. Publishers like getting one main title suggestion and two or three alternates you also feel might be appropriate.

MISTAKE #19
Not Painting a Picture of the Book in Chapter One

Too often authors jump in with the first step of a program or analyzing a problem in Chapter One. But that's getting off on the wrong foot. The first chapter of your book is your opportunity to introduce and articulate the key themes of your book, to paint a picture of what it offers the reader. That's why you should begin with a chapter that establishes the book's theme and purpose – one that provides the reader an overview of what you have to say. Describe what it will encompass, what readers can expect to learn and how the book will benefit them. Preview the elements, chapters and techniques to come. Hint: Don't call it "Overview," which sounds academic and vague. Give it an interesting title, as with all chapters.

Envision Chapter One as your entire book boiled down to the length of a magazine article. Write it exactly as if you were trying to convey the basics of the book to a friend over lunch.

MISTAKE #20
Lack of an Introductory Overview Paragraph in Every Chapter

Too often, novice writers, eager to get started, plunge into the meat of their chapter without pausing to orient the reader first. They begin by disabusing readers of some misconception about an obscure aspect of the subject. Or they immediately begin describing the cause of a problem, without first telling the reader that there is a problem under discussion, or what the problem is. Or they delve into some key element of an esoteric and undefined umbrella issue without taking the time to explicitly state the connections to the subject at hand.

Because you know your subject inside and out, you may assume that whoever reads your book will also be familiar with the larger context or subject. But this is not the case, or they wouldn't need your book in the first place. If you plunge off into the deep woods of your subject, you may leave your readers lost and stranded behind you. A clear introductory paragraph is a way to place a compass in their hands, so they can see their way clearly and follow your line of reasoning with greater confidence.

I find it easier to keep the chapters of my own books on track if I write a paragraph, at either the very start or immediately following a catchy opening, that gives an overview of the chapter's theme and subject matter. I believe every author should make this a conscious practice – and follow it religiously in every chapter. Be sure you encompass all of your chapter's ideas and promises.

You want to create a clear, succinct statement of the problem, cause or solution, addressed directly to "you" (the reader). Then provide a hint of the promise that all of that can change, how it can change for the better, and the reason why it can change. What's wanted is a very simple but concrete description.

For example: "This chapter offers a three-step technique for overcoming the destructive effects that being bullied as a child can have on your self-esteem. Bullying can be even more devastating than ostracism when you are a child because of the added element of physical threat, either implied or overt."

This helps you, and the reader, to stay focused on the issues at hand.

MISTAKE #21
Not Linking Each Chapter to the Book's Theme and Previous Chapters

This is another case where being too familiar with your subject can lead you to assume the reader will automatically make connections you haven't explicitly explained. The relationship between your book's theme and the theme of the chapter you are writing may seem to go without saying to you. But to the harried, distracted reader, who doesn't have the hours or years of research and experience that you do, the connection might not be so intuitive. As always, err on the side of caution. Take a sentence or two at the beginning of each chapter to illuminate how it follows the one that preceded it; or at the end of the chapter, to explain how it leads into the next.

Also take the time to explain why you placed the chapter where it is in the book. Usually authors have a reason for the order in which they present their chapters. In a how-to book, where you are presenting a ten-step program, you would probably have a good reason for the order of the steps. For instance, in a book about recovering from substance abuse, your first chapter might be about "acceptance," because you believe that none of the other steps work if someone hasn't genuinely accepted that they are addicted. The second chapter might focus on joining a recovery group, because you don't believe it is possible to work any of the other steps alone. And so forth.

To recap: Take a sentence or two. Explain why the chapter comes where it does, plus how and why it follows the preceding chapter. If you don't, the reader may be confused. Taking the time to explicitly connect the steps in your program can make the relationship between the steps clearer, and make it easier for the reader to remember their sequence.

MISTAKE #22
Not Sticking to a Strong Chapter Structure

Sometimes chapters sprawl. Writers, knowing their subject in detail, don't know where to start or where to stop. Novice writers may not have a sense of which aspects of their subject deserve expansive treatment and which need only a brief mention. They may spend too much time on non-essential details, or fail to provide their readers with key information. An author may, for example, mean to describe a problem and offer a solution. But without realizing it, she or he ends up writing entirely about the nature of a problem and forgets to address what can be done to remedy it.

If you are primarily writing a book that tackles a problem and offers a solution – from a better golf stroke to increased brain power – keep in mind the following chapter structure:

1. Introduce subject of chapter
2. Establish/describe the problem
3. Describe the remedy/solution

When you have finished a chapter, review it to determine if you have devoted sufficient space to each of these three sections.

MISTAKE #23
Not Getting to the Subject of a Chapter Immediately

There's something wrong with a chapter if readers find themselves halfway through it before the ostensible subject blazoned in the chapter title is mentioned. If a chapter focuses on self-esteem and body image, it should dive into that subject within a page or two. If you go five to seven pages and haven't begun writing about self-esteem and body image, either change the title and theme of your chapter so they correspond to what you have written, or start the chapter over and get to the subject quicker.

MISTAKE #24
Infrequent Use of Headings and Subheadings

Not using headings to enliven chapters and break them down into easily digestible chunks can kill sales and make readers give up on your book long before the end. Without headings, it can be hard for readers to:

* Identify your key ideas
* See the "progression" of a chapter
* Easily relocate material when they want to refer back to it later

Conversely, headings do all three of the above. That's why frequent use of headings is essential. Ideally, you should have a heading or subheading for each new idea or topic within a chapter. Each heading should reflect the theme or message of the material that follows. These headings act as markers to keep the reader focused on your themes, and to highlight the key issues, making them easier for the reader to spot.

For example, in a chapter about "running in the Zone," some of the material might be about the speed at which one runs when "in the Zone." Other material might be about various other names by which the state known as "being in the Zone" has been called, like "peak performance," "the burn," etc. Still other material might offer evidence that you, too, can learn to "run in the Zone." Preface each of these sections with a heading like "Unbelievable Speed," or "What's In a Name," or "You Can Do It Too!" Do this and you can see how easy it would be for the reader to stay on track with your message and relocate the material later.

MISTAKE #25
Failure to Introduce Each Section Within a Chapter

Beneath each heading you should have an introductory paragraph – doing for the section under the heading what the introductory paragraph does for your chapter. State the section's basic idea, why it is important, why it follows the preceding section, etc. All of this re-hashing may feel repetitive to you, the expert author. But your goal here is to be both persuasive and clear. Giving your readers little signposts to guide them through your argument or program helps to reassure them of your competence and expertise. It's like white-water rafting. Everyone feels more relaxed with a confident, experienced guide who takes the time to prepare them for what's ahead.

MISTAKE #26
Failure to Use Bulleted Lists

Too often beginning authors scorn the use of bulleted lists as being unneccessary decoration, or as a way of over-simplifying and talking down to readers. Both of these misconceptions could not be further from the truth. Bulleted lists serve a very important purpose: They help you put your thoughts across to readers by calling attention to a series of ideas, relationships, steps, or facts, and by highlighting key points. This helps readers remember them and makes it easier for readers to find things they want to look up later for reference and review.

Reread the preceding sentence. It contains three key facts – the reasons why the use of bulleted lists is so crucial. But these three reasons are buried in the middle of the text. They are the key elements in the material around them, but they don't stand out clearly from the surrounding text. There is nothing about them that cries out, "Notice me!" in any way. Plus, surrounded as the sentence is by other text, it would be difficult for readers to locate quickly if they wanted to reread it or look it up.

But imagine how those three concepts jump off the page when you rearrange the same sentence in the form of a bulleted list. It will help you put your thoughts across to readers by:

  * Calling attention to series of ideas, relationships, steps, facts

* Highlighting key ideas so the reader is more likely to remember them
* Making it easier for readers to locate things they want to look up later for reference and review

Also use bullets to preview the key ideas in a chapter or a subsection of a chapter. This way, readers will find it easier to follow the main points of the section and keep the topics to be covered in mind. They will also know where they can find a guide to what you, the author, consider the salient points. Tie the headings in your text to the elements in your lists. This will reinforce your key ideas and impress them more deeply in the reader's mind. Hint: If you include something in a list, be sure to cover it somewhere in the chapter. Oddly enough, writers sometimes neglect to do this. Anything worth highlighting in a list is probably worth elaborating on somewhere later in your chapter.

MISTAKE #27
Failure to Bring Each Chapter to a Formal Conclusion

Finally, you can't go wrong by ending each chapter – and each section within it – with a concluding or summarizing paragraph or two. This is where you recap what you consider the most important ideas, the ones you most want the reader to remember. You might also want to include a note of hope into the conclusion, and a bit about the next chapter and how it relates to the present one.

It might look something like this: "Now you know the most common errors of chapter construction: failure to introduce your chapters, failure to stick to the subject, failure to introduce subsections within chapters, etc. In the future, you can tackle your own chapters with confidence and greater effectiveness, knowing your work will be free of these pitfalls. Now it's time to..."

MISTAKE #28
Making Chapters Too Long or Too Short

Chapters that are significantly longer or shorter than average undercut the effectiveness of your book. When a chapter is too long, readers begin to become restless, or even quit reading altogether. When a chapter is too short, readers may feel as if there is no substance to it, as if they are being short-changed.

What's a good length for a chapter? Generally, the best chapters run anywhere from ten to thirty-five manuscript pages (about 5000 - 7000 words). Fifteen to forty pages is a good range. When you have chapters that are too short, look for ways to meld them together; conversely, try to break over-lengthy ones into two (or more!) chapters.

PART FOUR
MISTAKES IN
WRITING & STYLE

Style in writing is like sex in marriage. There may be more to a relationship than sex. But sex is what attracted you in the first place, and it's the cement that keeps things going. The better your style, the deeper and longer lasting the relationship. In this section you will learn how to avoid the mistakes that can end your relationship with readers almost before it begins.

MISTAKE #29
Failure to Write in an Everyday, Easy-to-Understand Style

Too often authors use language that is dry, academic, indirect, or impersonal. Here's one such example from a book on Adult Children of Alcoholics: "All these destructive behavior patterns have arisen of course as the result of dysfunctional family processes internalized during the childhood stage of development."

This is writing from the outside, analyzing the reader and their problems from one or two removes, as in an academic study. Terms like "dysfunctional behavior patterns" distance the readers, making them think that you see them as mere case histories. It destroys that direct, personal connection that keeps readers interested in your book.

It's also a turn-off in another way: It ends up going far over the average person's head. Most people don't habitually think in this kind of language or in sentences of this length. It reads like a college textbook, not a work written for the average woman or man in the street.

When readers think of themselves and their problems, they don't think in terms of academic or abstract phrases. They think in the same kind of normal, everyday words they use when they speak.

Unfortunately, academics are trained not to think this way, and many experts – from fitness training to peak performance – tend to think in terms of the jargon of their specialty. They assume that everyone will understand the specialized terms and abbreviations they use with colleagues or fellow-enthusiasts. Even when they think they are writing in everyday terms, they are not.

Strive for a direct, personal, casual writing style in your own work. Recast academic phraseology and abstract ideas or suggestions in concrete terms, in the context of how it affects the readers' lives.

Publisher Jeremy Tarcher offers excellent advice for simplifying and translating your ideas into everyday language. Use the kinds of normal, conversational words and phrases the people around you typically use when talking about themselves. This kind of writing strikes an immediate chord in a reader and establishes that vital, emotional connection with a book. Jeremy used to say one way to capture this style is to picture yourself at a party in casual conversation with a stranger who expresses interest when they hear about the subject of your book. Imagine how you would explain it to them – then write it that way. Tarcher calls it the "conversational style." Hint: Many articles for popular magazines are written in this style. Pick up one and study the way magazine writers phrase things.

Here is how the sentence ("All these destructive behavior patterns have arisen of course as the result of dysfunctional family processes internalized during the childhood stage of development.") might be recast in the conversational style: "The fact that you explode into uncontrollable anger, drink to hide from your problems, drift from one superficial relationship to another, and engage in other self-destructive behaviors is the direct result of having seen your alcoholic parent do the same thing when you were a child."

Hint: Passive tenses create boring, remote prose that distances readers. Examples: "She had been abused by her dad," versus "Her dad abused her." Or, rather than, "He was crippled by depression," say, "Depression crippled him." Or, rather than, "Doing your exercises every day will make you stronger," write, "Exercising every day makes you stronger." The later examples are crisp, immediate, and more involving.

MISTAKE #30
Lack of Topic Sentences

Another common mistake among novice authors is to plunge into a paragraph without stopping to provide the classic topic sentence. You probably remember the idea of the topic sentence – our teachers tried to drill them into our heads back in middle school and high school. The topic sentence is nothing more or less than a description of the basic theme or point of the paragraph.

Without a topic sentence to guide them, readers may become confused about the true focus of a paragraph. They may not understand the point of the paragraph, or only grasp it at the end. Knowing the paragraph's focus at the beginning provides a context that helps the reader retain more of its ideas and content. This paragraph, for example, begins with a topic sentence.

Hint: Of course, if you work on a computer, you don't have to write the topic sentence first. I often find that I write a better one *after* I finish writing a paragraph, because I have a keener sense of the paragraph's theme and contents.

MISTAKE #31
Using the Wrong Word Instead of the Right One

Mark Twain once wrote: "The difference between the almost right word and the right word is really a large matter—'tis the difference between the lightning-bug and the lightning." Of course, when you are in the white-hot throes of inspiration, there is not always time to stop and search for the precise word to express your ideas. But later, during the revision process, a little time looking it up in a thesaurus is time well spent. Never underestimate the power of the right word both to communicate your meaning more clearly and to stick like a burr in the reader's mind so they never forget your message. Conversely, never underestimate the power of the wrong word to obscure your meaning, confuse the issue, and rob your work of memorability.

Language is a tool that you can use to get across your meaning. Take this sentence: "She held his hand." It seems simple enough, but it's pretty vague. There's not really a lot going on there. What if "She gripped his hand" instead? Now we've got a story. Or "She caressed his hand." Now something entirely different is happening. Again, don't stress about it in the rough draft stage – just get those words out there and on the paper. But if you're at the point where you are pitching your manuscript to publishers, you should take the time to see if there are places where you can improve your language.

Take time now to double-check that your intended meaning is coming across. Make sure you don't say that mice make you "shutter" (are you a house?) if you mean that they make you "shudder." Are you on the lookout for "rouge" golf balls (are they wearing makeup?) or "rogue" balls? And are you in the "mist" of an argument, or in the "midst" of it? Or take the phrase, "He had the wealth of Midas." While there is nothing wrong with this sentence, neither is there much right with it, wordwise. A more specific word here would be "possessed" or "owned" or "amassed." Just substitute any of these words in that sentence and see how much fuller and more powerful it sounds.

MISTAKE #32
Using Vague Pronouns that Could Refer to Anything

Sometimes when you are writing a chapter or section of your book, the subject at hand seems so obvious that it doesn't seem necessary to mention it more than once. Having established that you are talking about money market funds, you use pronouns like "them" and "they. Or, having mentioned "Carol X.," you simply refer to her as "her" or "she."

The problem with relying solely on vague pronouns – like "it," "his," "they," etc. – is that they could stand for anything. As a result, after a few sentences or paragraphs, readers are left mentally up a tree. They lose track of the original subject and end up wondering just what the heck you are talking about.

Take the following sentence: "It came at him." What was "it?" Who was "he?" If "it" was a mouse and "he" a cat, it (the sentence) has one meaning; if the other way around, the meaning is considerably different.

Among the pronouns that can turn treacherously nonspecific are:

she
he
it
they

those
them
any
some

To eliminate the confusion caused by overuse of pronouns, explicitly name the subject you are writing about at least once in every paragraph. That gives your readers something to hold onto, and helps them to keep a clear idea of what you are talking about. Hint: Your subject will usually be a person, place or thing.

MISTAKE #33
Use of Overly Abstract Language

It is easy to think you are communicating an idea because *you* know what you mean, when your phrasing is actually very abstract. As a result, language that conveys an image clearly to you, may convey very little to the reader. For instance, take the following sentence from a book on tapping into "inner guidance": *The next pages will help set your mind at ease, freeing you to move forward by offering you the sympathy and support you deserve in regard to what has led you astray from your Inner Guide and blocked you from full access to your capacity for so long.*

See what I mean about writing being too abstract? There isn't one concrete fact or image in this sentence so far. It meant something to its author, but likely it left you with a few questions. Let's break it down and look at it a phrase at a time: *The next pages will help set your mind at ease* [about what?], *freeing you to move forward* [in what sense? Toward? What does this mean?] *by offering you the sympathy and support you deserve* [huh? explain, please!] *in regard to what has led you astray* [could this be more indirect?] *from your Inner Guide and blocked you from full access to your capacity for so long.*

Hint: Review your work for vague, indirect phraseology. Replace it with more concrete, specific language.

MISTAKE #34
Failure to Rein-In Run-On Sentences

Studies show most readers can easily and quickly assimilate sentences of between twelve and eighteen words in length. Sentences of more than eighteen words – or about two lines – either slow them down and require rereading, or get misunderstood. Run-on sentences of more than say, three lines, or about twenty-four words, give readers the most difficulty.

If you want to communicate in an easily understood style, rein-in your run-on sentences. Keep your words focused and to the point. Review your final manuscript and rewrite any sentences you find that are three lines or longer into two shorter ones. Hint: Look for commas and semicolons that could be turned into periods.

MISTAKE #35
Using Overly Wordy Writing

Crisp, to-the-point sentences compel reader interest. The unnecessary use or employment of overly verbose words and phrases can prove tiresome, causing reader interest to dwindle or altogether die. Or, perhaps I should follow my own advice and say here instead, "Using too many words makes readers tune out."

See the difference?

Always review what you have written for verbose sections with unnecessary words and phrases. Tighten the sentences by removing the inessential words. Remember, the more pointed the sentence, the more likely the reader is to get the point. Hint: If you can say it with one word instead of with three, without changing the meaning, you should.

MISTAKE #36
Failure to Define Professional, Trade and Technical Terms

You know the meanings of the technical/professional terms and phrases you use when you write about the subject of your book. But, though dense with meaning to you, these words may not be as meaningful to lay readers. For example, in a golf book, beginners may not be familiar with terms like "slice," "hook," "follow-through," etc. Or in a book on recovering from sex addiction, words and phrases like "inner child," "codependent," even "recovery" itself, may be new to those just beginning their quest for healing. Advanced knitters may know all about a "kitchener stitch bind-off" or "circular intarsia," but the rest of us are going to need a little more explanation.

When should you define a word or phrase, and when can you assume it's something everyone will be familiar with? A good rule is to define every technical, professional or academic word you use. If any turn out to be unnecessary, your editor can delete them from the final text. Hint: Err on the side of safety and define, define, define.

MISTAKE #37
Using Negative Comparisons

Another serious reader turn-off is describing something in terms of what it "isn't." When you put it that way, it seems silly. The very definition of "description" is a summarizing of what something "is."

Yet, far too often, writers fall into exactly that trap. I once edited a manuscript on meditation whose author devoted the first chapter to explaining what meditation wasn't. Unfortunately, the author neglected to explain what meditation was. When this failing was pointed out, she immediately revised the chapter and devoted the majority of the space to detailing what meditation is – without relying solely on negative comparisons.

Here are some typical examples. From a biography: "The café to which he led her was hardly splendid. Inside, they ordered spaghetti and Chianti."

Well, exactly what was that café like? "Hardly splendid" hardly conjures a specific image. Between "splendid" restaurants and the lowest dive, there is a wide range of possible dining establishments.

Or, "Being 'in the Zone' doesn't mean working like a robot." Or, "Love addiction doesn't mean you just like to be in relationships." Alone, these tell us nothing about what these conditions are. They cry out for an explanation of what they are – not just what they aren't.

Why do writers sometimes unwittingly describe things in terms of what they aren't, instead of vice versa? Often, when you are an expert, you become very aware of the many misconceptions people have about your subject. In a book on meditation you might want to counter the mistaken belief that meditation is a form of self-hypnosis, or that it is a religious ritual, or that it is some kind of self-induced "high." Naturally, you want to disabuse the reader of these misconceptions. So you write that "meditation isn't self-hypnosis," "meditation isn't a religious ritual," "meditation isn't a self-induced 'high.'"

This gets you off on the wrong foot in two respects. It gets you focused on what something isn't – so much so that you may forget to write about what it is. The second is that this approach to alerting readers to common misconceptions is so indirect that they may not realize what you are trying to do, and retain their misconception.

Of course, when coupled with a positive description of your subject, negative comparisons can be helpful. You might write, "Rather than meditation being like a hypnotic trance, it is like relaxing completely in a lawn chair on a summer day."

Negative comparisons are unavoidable when it is necessary to counter myths and misunderstandings about your subject. But, be sure you tackle the subject explicitly. Write a heading like "10 Misconceptions about Karate." Then address the reader directly with something like, "You've probably been exposed to a number of misconceptions about Karate. These may include..." Finally, write a paragraph explaining why each is a fallacy.

MISTAKE #38
Failure to Write the Reader into the Book

When you're writing about behaviors and problems shared by many people, it is easy to lose sight of the individual reader who has purchased your book, has taken it home and is reading it. You can get in the habit of writing your book in terms of "people," "others," "individuals" or in categories like "addicts," "gymnasts," "adult children of alcoholics." When you write about these groups or people, you believe that what you are writing about applies to each specific reader, and you naturally expect the reader to make the same connection.

However, the reader may not see themselves in words like "individuals" or "adult children of alcoholics." Readers typically believe that anyone who succeeds, recovers, launches their own business, or becomes a better tennis player, is somehow special and different. They may not see their own ordinary lives as possibly being a part of that success story. And sometimes, when readers are tired or distracted, they may simply fail to make the connection between their own lives and the abstract group you are talking about.

When readers fail to see themselves in a self-help book, it turns them off in two ways: The prose feels cold, remote and objective to them, lacking the sense of personal connection that keeps someone excited and reading. Secondly, they don't have the all-vital sense that they are learning what they want to know. The reader may still believe that your ideas are valid. But it will feel to them as if your book were standing at one remove, analyzing their problem instead of seeing it from the inside – the way they see and experience the problem.

The easiest way to solve this is to avoid writing in terms of other people and abstract groups altogether. Instead, address your book directly to the reader by using the word "you" frequently, essentially in every paragraph, several times. This way the reader can't miss seeing themselves in your book, and feeling a connection to its subject matter. Hint: If you've gone several pages without writing "you," something is wrong. Really, if you go more than three paragraphs without it, or if you don't find yourself using it several times in a paragraph or sentence – as I do here – you are off-track and need to get back on.

Let's say you are a psychotherapist specializing in dream interpretation, writing a book on the topic. You could begin by describing the typical client who comes to you, the dreams they have, and something about how you help or advise them, etc. But this is remote, and the reader may not think of themselves as typical or see the relevance to themselves. Don't leave it to the reader to make this connection on their own. Instead of writing, "A typical person generally dreams about..." write, "You probably have the same dreams as most people, such as..." Or, "Do these dreams seem familiar to you? If so, relax; you're normal."

By bringing the reader and the problems which

drew them to this book farther on stage this way, you create the vital emotional connection with your material that makes a bestseller.

MISTAKE #39
Writing More About Yourself than the Reader

Another big reader turn-off is writing too much about yourself in your book. Of course, if you're writing an autobiography, that's one thing. But if your aim is to offer readers something that can help improve their lives, then keep the focus on them and off of you.

You may think of yourself as pretty ordinary. You figure that by using yourself as an example, the reader will realize that if you can do it, they can do it. But often readers will see you as someone far superior to them, someone born with the lucky genes necessary to become the success or expert you are. You're the one who could write a whole book on this, right? It may not dawn on them that what works for you will work for them as well.

Putting too much about you, your thoughts and experiences, into your manuscript, can turn readers away. Readers may feel ignored, as if the book is more of an autobiography than a how-to book about them and their concerns. Surveys show that many readers are turned off by books when they see the word "I" too often. They tend to think of the author as an egotist or braggart.

You may think it is necessary to use "I" to remind readers of your experience and credentials, but this isn't true. You have already provided them with the most convincing credential of all – your book.

Stick with writing directly to the reader and putting things in terms of their experiences, rather than your own, and save your story for your book's Preface.

PART FIVE
PRESENTING THE STEPS OR ELEMENTS OF YOUR PROGRAM

If chapters are the meat of your manuscript, then the heart of it is the chapters that present the actual steps, techniques and elements that make yours a how-to/self-help book. If they aren't easy for readers to understand and try out, all of your efforts will be for nothing. Keep these chapters clear and organized, with the steps and exercises spelled out in detail, and your book will be well on its way toward the bestseller lists.

MISTAKE #40
Inconsistent Formatting

When it comes to introducing the individual programmatic chapters and subsections of your book (such as the Seven Steps to Recovery or the Six Characteristics of a Thriving Organization), it is essential that you find a fully consistent way to present them. Inconsistency in a book distracts readers, and you don't want readers distracted by the book's formatting when they should be absorbing its content.

Don't present a bulleted list of the steps in some exercises, and omit such lists for other exercises. Don't use anecdotes to illustrate how people develop key problems associated with being adult children of alcoholics in some chapters, and not use any anecdotes in other chapters. Don't give exercises for developing some skills, and forget to provide exercises for other skills. Don't number the steps of an exercise in one spot and use letters for the steps in other spots – or if you have a good reason for doing so, warn the reader in the Preface to your book.

Instead, develop a consistent format for each element – and stick to it. If you use any of the above once, use them all the time.

MISTAKE #41
Failure to Explicitly State the Problem at the Beginning

There's no point in plunging into the solution to a problem unless you have first told the reader what the problem is. Perhaps the problem, say, Compulsive Spending, is identified in the chapter title or section heading. So it may not seem necessary to restate it before an exercise. Or perhaps the problem being addressed seems so apparent to you, as the author, that you assume it will be equally apparent to everyone else. Typically, however, readers don't see the connection at all. Instead, they become so confused they may not keep reading until they finally figure out the problem from the context.

Open any section of your book that focuses on problem-solving with an explicit statement of the problem being solved. Then, and only then, you can proceed to the specific prescription for solving it. Not only will this approach prevent the reader from becoming lost, it will also help you keep your own eye on the ball of the prescriptive.

MISTAKE #42
Using the Same Opening "Hook" Every Time

Formatting consistency doesn't mean every time you introduce a programmatic section, you should do it the same way. Don't use repetitive constructions. Don't begin each section with the same kind of opening sentence or paragraph. Don't start them all with "Many..." with "Like so many people today..." or "Josephina, who always seemed to..." Don't start them all with "Don'ts." That will bore the reader, and they may stop reading.

Here are some examples of different literary gambits you can use for keeping your opening paragraphs alive and interesting. Try:

"Many people have difficulty with..."
"Mary, like so many people today..."
"One of the most common relationship difficulties is..."
"If you are like many people today, you may have trouble with..."
"Have you ever experienced..."
"Does this sound like something that has happened to you..."
"Or whatever other variants the author's fertile brain concocts..."

MISTAKE #43
Not Using a New Heading to Highlight Each Step of Your Program or Exercises

What you don't call attention to, readers won't notice. You want readers to come away remembering the key elements of your program, or the key steps in an exercise. You can be confident they will if you type a heading for every new step or technique. This may even mean having one or more headings per page. Giving each key element its own heading helps call attention to it, making it likelier to be noticed and remembered.

MISTAKE #44
Not Creating Unique Formatting that Captures Reader Imagination

Take a look at the best-selling "Complete Idiot's Guide" or "For Dummies" books. You will see that each series has created unique formatting elements – like important ideas summarized in a small box to so that they stand out, or cute icons like a smiling face for how-to tips and a frowning face for "don'ts." Readers love these! Unique formatting elements help readers quickly locate important material and key ideas – and they're fun.

The Complete Idiot's Guide books successfully appeal to readers by combining boxed material and icons. Typically there are four types of boxes in this series: one focused on Definitions, one focused on Tips about how to do things, one focused on Warnings, one focused on Intriguing Facts about the subject most people don't know. In the case of the *CIG to Evolution*, all the boxes highlighting definitions of key terms are headed by a cute drawing of a platypus reading a dictionary, while boxed material containing a two or three sentence profile of a famous scientist is headed by a cartoon bust of Darwin.

Unique formatting doesn't have to mean expensive graphics. A simple device, deployed consistently, may be enough to "brand" your book and burn your ideas into reader's memories. In Doreen Virtue's book, *Divine Prescriptions*, which presented angelic advice for earthly problems in life, love and business, a major formatting element was a little prescription symbol (Rx.) followed by an italicized summation of the prescription. It looked something like the following: "Rx.: Sometimes we prevent ourselves from meeting our ideal soulmate because what we consciously believe would be the perfect partner for us isn't our ideal kind of soulmate at all. Ask the angels to bring you the right person, and be open to recognizing that person, however different they may seem from your ideal."

Hint: Review other books and then dream up some unique formatting elements to spice up your book!

MISTAKE #45
Failure to Make Instructions Direct and To the Point

You may think a statement like, "I recommend the use of light hand weights to build up your arms for hockey," conveys a clear instruction to the reader. But the reader may not understand what you're talking about at all.

In order to understand you, the reader actually has to go through a number of mental processes. First, they have to realize you are implying something, and then they have to figure out what it is.

This mental process is called an abstraction. And if someone is reading hurriedly or in distracting surroundings – yelling kids, blaring television, someone shouting from the kitchen – they may miss your implication and keep reading, never realizing that there was an indirect instruction implied in your phraseology. Even if they do grasp the hint that anyone who wants to play hockey can benefit from the use of hand weights, they may not make the connection to themselves and realize you mean that they could benefit, too.

Eliminate the possibility of the reader missing your valuable advice altogether. Explicitly tell them to do something, and how to do it. For instance, "Begin exercising daily with hand weights. This builds up your muscles for hockey." (Then give step-by-step instructions for exercises they should do with the weights, and for how long.)

MISTAKE #46
Not Fully Explaining Exercises Before Presenting Them

Another common error is to simply present an exercise with a title (and sometimes without even that!). The author who does this makes two mistakes: First, they overestimate how easy it will be to entice readers into doing the exercise. Second, they assume the reader will deduce what the exercise is for.

Readers are notoriously reluctant to try exercises. They lack confidence in their own abilities, and are certain that even if they do try an exercise, they will find it difficult and taxing. They are also reluctant to invest their time in any activity unless they know beforehand that there is something in it for them.

In order to motivate readers to try the exercises you offer, you need to preface all exercises with a paragraph or several that put the carrot on the stick and make clear what's in it for them. Always address these four key issues before you present any exercise:

1. The problem or lack of ability it remedies.
2. The promise. How it will benefit the reader. How it solves the problem or what new skill it teaches.
3. How and why the exercise works. The

premise or idea behind it. What makes it effective.
4. That it is easy to learn.

In a book on marketing, for example, you might have an exercise called: "Coining 'Sell Phrases'" that would be introduced something like this: "Most people think they can't coin the same kind of dynamic, sizzling 'sell phrases' that advertising and marketing geniuses do. But they are wrong. You can learn to produce the exact same kind of 'sell phrases' on demand, every time you need them. You already have the ability. If you are able to talk to other people so that they understand you, all you need to learn is a simple, six-step process for coining 'sell phrases' that draws on your own ability to use words."

MISTAKE #47
Not Spelling Out Exercises in Numbered Steps

Writing good exercises is an art. When you have a clear image of an exercise, it's easy to feel that the elements are self-explanatory, and that actually labeling them Step 1, Step 2, etc. would be redundant. But it's not redundant – it's a necessity.

Generally, an exercise teaches readers a new ability they didn't have before. Or it may fine-tune a skill that they already possess, but aren't making the best use of. Both situations intimidate readers. Most people are certain they have unusual difficulty learning and will get things wrong. They can literally panic when they find advice or tips that haven't been broken down into numbered steps. They immediately become confused and trip themselves up trying to think of every possible interpretation of what you've written. In all these cases, they are more likely to give up than to give your techniques a try.

But there's no guesswork when you format your exercises in the form of numbered steps. Using them relieves the reader's feelings of intimidation. Plus, since the exercise has been divided into small, easy sections, readers become more confident that they can do it. The result is that readers are far more likely to give your exercises a try.

In short, don't just write down your exercises in the form of general advice. Take for example, the following exercise for coining dramatic, colorful "sell" phrases. Here's what not to do: "Write down what you want to say in your own words. Rephrase what you have written to give it as positive a spin as possible. Using what you have just written as inspiration, dream up four or five other positive ways you might formulate your point. Go over everything you have written, including your first, rough try at what you wanted to say. Underline, or put a check mark next to, the words you think have the most power. Try putting the words you have underlined together in different creative combinations. Write down the results. Pick several possibilities, compare them with the six criteria for a power phrase (dramatic and vivid, easily pictured or understood, a bold statement, important information or a call to action, interest-piquing, concise and succinct)."

You can see why just presenting the information as general advice in the form of a normal paragraph could be difficult to follow. But notice how much more quickly and clearly you can assimilate the basic idea of the exercise when it's spelled out step by step. Take this example from the hypothetical exercise on "Coining 'Sell Phrases'":

Step 1. Write down what you want to say in your own words.

Step 2. Rephrase what you have written to give it as positive a spin as possible.

Step 3. Using what you have just written as inspiration, dream up four or five other positive ways you might formulate your point.

Step 4. Go over everything you have written, including your first, rough try at what you wanted to say. Underline or put a check mark next to the words you think have the most power.

Step 5. Try putting the words you have underlined together in different creative combinations. Write down the results.

Step 6. Pick several possibilities, compare them with the six criteria for a power phrase – 1) dramatic and vivid, 2) easily pictured or understood, 3) a bold statement, 4) important information or a call to action, 5) interest-piquing, 6) concise and succinct.

MISTAKE #48
Not Illustrating How Each Step Works

It isn't enough to describe an abstract step. Readers will have difficulty visualizing them. Instead, provide examples of what it is like to do each step. This will give readers a more concrete idea of what you mean. They will be both more likely to risk trying them, and will find them easier. Take the example on "sell phrases" used above. This is one way it might be amplified to give the reader a more concrete picture of how the steps work:

Step 1. Write down what you want to say in your own words. Hint: Set down the first words that come to mind (it doesn't matter how awkward or inadequate they feel). You might write something like, "Reduce the errors my department is making to zero and eliminate defects."

Step 2. Rephrase what you have written to give it as positive a spin as possible. For example, "Get it 100% right."

Step 3. Using what you have just written as inspiration, dream up four or five other positive ways you might formulate your point. You might write, "Get more quality in quality control," and "No tolerance for errors."

Step 4. Go over everything you have written, including your first, rough try at what you wanted to say. Put a check mark next to the phrases you think have the most power. (Unless something you have written already looks like an ideal candidate for a power phrase; in which case, skip the next two steps and go straight to the checklist below.) For example, you might put a check next to the following phrases you wrote: "Reduce errors to zero and eliminate defects." "Get it 100% right," "Get more quality in quality control," and "No tolerance for errors."

Step 5. Try putting the words you have underlined together in different creative combinations. Write down the results. You might end up with phrases like, "100% quality," "Zero tolerance," "Control defects," "Zero tolerance for defects," "Adding the quality to quality control," "Control quality, Zero defects," or "100% quality, 100% of the time," etc.

Step 6. Pick several possibilities, compare them with the six criterion for a power phrase – is it: 1) dramatic and vivid, 2) easily pictured or understood, 3) making a bold statement, 4) presenting important information or a call to action, 5) interest-piquing, 6) concise and succinct?

MISTAKE #49
Making Exercises Overly Lengthy or Complicated

The KISS rule (Keep It Simple, Stupid!) applies to exercises too. Overly complicated or lengthy exercises are still the KISS of death for your book. Long-winded descriptions tire readers out, as well as leaving them confused and feeling worse about themselves. If they encounter even one such exercise, most readers will give up on it, your program and your book.

Here are some guidelines for keeping your exercises simple, so you won't look stupid:

* Keep the number of steps low. A ten-step exercise is pushing it. Six to eight is a good upper limit. A dozen or more steps is far too complicated.

* Keep the time it takes to do exercises low. Five minutes is a good length! Ten to twenty minutes is reasonable. But, if an exercise takes thirty minutes or more, it is too long!

MISTAKE #50
Failure to Sum-Up Exercises

All too often, after presenting an excellent exercise, authors simply stop after giving the last step and go on to a new topic. They don't take the time to show how to use the insights generated, or explain what situations may be tackled with these new skills. This leaves readers feeling empty-handed and confused.

Once again, you have fallen prey to the cardinal blunder of expertise. You, the expert, know how to interpret such experiences and the kinds of insights reviewing them can generate. But, this is another instance where you assume wrongly that the reader already knows what you are trying to teach them. If the reader were used to the process and knew what the results meant, then she or he wouldn't need your book!

This is a case where more is more, not less. Take a few paragraphs after each and every one of your exercises to explain how the reader can make use of the insights generated. Take, for instance, an exercise that involves recalling figures and incidents from childhood which contributed to the reader's feelings of inadequacy. Give the reader some reassurace or direction after this experience, to help them deal with the feelings that may have been generated. Or, if your book teaches skills, say, intimacy skills like communicating with a partner in "I" statements, take a paragraph and point out what kinds of situations call upon these skills and what kind of results they might expect.

PART SIX
MISTAKES IN USING QUOTATIONS & CASE HISTORIES

Quotations from the writings of other authorities on your subject, and case histories (aka personal stories or anecdotes), are essential ingredients in most self-help/how-to books. These help illustrate and reinforce your points. Yet, helpful as they are, they can also prove to be pitfalls. If not used correctly, they may confuse rather than illuminate the reader.

MISTAKE #51
Over- or Under-relying on Quotes from Authorities

You're the expert in the reader's eyes, after all they are holding a book you hae written and someone found it worthy of publishing. For the most part, the reader will believe anything you say about your subject. However, readers become even more confident about accepting your ideas and suggestions when they know other experts have reached the same conclusions. Research shows using quotes from various other writers that echo what you have said helps your ideas really stand out! So most publishers recommend you cite a supportive or illustrative quotation from another book or magazine article every two to four pages. You want one that essentially says the same thing you are saying, in slightly different words. These are not hard to find, and you have probably noted dozens in reading about your own field of expertise. (Scattering quotations throughout your manuscript like this also helps show readers that you've done your homework and are as widely read on the subject as they expect an expert to be.)

Conversely, some writers fail to put enough of themselves and their thoughts into their books. Instead, they mistakenly rely on long passages of quotations to make their points, and only supply a sentence or so here and there to connect one quote with another. Generally, this makes it difficult for readers to be certain what subject or theme the various batches of quotes illustrate. It also makes it seem as if you don't have any ideas of your own. Instead, you should subordinate the quotations to your own writing, using a quotation no more often than every page or so.

MISTAKE #52
Not Highlighting the Points of Quotations

The connection between what you have written and a relevant quotation from another author's work may be apparent to you. But don't assume it will be as apparent to the reader. Avoid just dropping a quotation into your text. Instead, preface it with an introductory sentence or phrase, explicitly summarizing its relevance. This way the reader will know what point they are to take away in relation to your own theme.

For example, let's say you have just written a paragraph about the belief shared by most weekend golfers that they can never play really well. Then you open the next paragraph with this quotation: "You have probably heard the saying that so-and-so is a 'born golfer,'" writes Josephina Doaks in her book, *Golfing the Natural Way*. "This misconception puts you in one category of player and the 'born golfer' in another – or so you think."

Now the significance of this quote, coming after what you have said about most weekend golfers believing they can never play really well, is open to interpretation. As a reader, I wonder if you meant to imply that the belief that weekend golfers can't play well is caused by the idea that some people are born "natural golfers" and some are not – I assume you place me in that category. Or you may mean to suggest that the belief that some are natural golfers and some are not keeps people from trying as hard as they might, and blocks them from realizing their full potential for playing the game. Or, you might mean to convey both ideas, or yet some other idea entirely.

But if you introduce the quotation with a sentence explaining how you feel the quote illuminates what you are saying in your book, you can be confident the reader will understand its full significance.

For instance: One reason most golfers think they can never play in the big leagues is that they think pros have some special ability the rest of us lack, as Josephina Doaks notes in her book *Golfing the Natural Way*. "You have probably heard the saying that so-and-so is a 'born golfer,'" Doaks writes. "This misconception puts you in one category of player and the 'born golfer' in another – or so you think."

MISTAKE #53
Failure to Illustrate Points with Anecdotes or Case Histories

It isn't enough to just describe your ideas, insights, techniques or strategies. Even the best description can still seem abstract or vague in the reader's mind. To make your ideas concrete and clear, you need to show your readers how they function in real-life scenarios.

Presenting real-life scenarios – also known as "case histories" and "anecdotes" – is the most powerful technique you can use to put your concepts across in a self-help book. Though the two terms are often used interchangeably (and are used that way in this book, too), there is a distinction between them. Case histories are just that, accounts from a professional's files telling the stories of clients with problems similar to the reader's. Anecdotes, rather than being about clients, are stories about other people the author knows or has read about that illustrate a book's ideas. Whatever you call them, they should appear frequently throughout you book. Otherwise it will feel dry and academic, and readers will have a difficult time picturing how your ideas translate to practical action. Hint: A minimum of one to three anecdotes or case histories per chapter is essential.

MISTAKE #54
Inconsistency in Anecdote Formatting

All too frequently, fledgling writers present case histories in their manuscript, which unintentionally ends up riddled with inconsistencies. Some of their anecdotes will have lengthy prefatory material before introducing the person the story is about. Others will begin by immediately jumping into an anecdote with little or no description of the subject at all. Sometimes the point of the anecdote will be spelled out. Other times, it won't. Sometimes there will be a paragraph or two after the anecdote detailing the solution to the problem and how it affected the clients' lives. Other times, case histories will lack this important bit of closure. To avoid distracting the reader, handle the formatting of all the case histories and other anecdotal material you present in the same way.

When in doubt, remember the most effective anecdotes contain the following five elements:

1. An explicit preview, in a sentence or two, of the point the case history will make
2. A thumbnail sketch of the person the story is about
3. The case history itself
4. Whether the person applied the techniques you suggest – and whether or not they helped
5. A follow-up recap of what you want the

reader to learn from the anecdote

Devote a paragraph or more to each of these elements and you will end up with the kind of illustrative anecdotes that highlight ideas, inspire readers and generate bestsellers. Hint: The ideal anecdote should probably average one to three pages long.

MISTAKE #55
Using Transcripts Rather than Case Histories

Never use transcripts of sessions with clients, or any other transcripts, in a book meant for a wide, popular readership. In other words, don't present any material in the following format:

Reader: Why not?

JMStine: Transcripts have a couple of shortcomings, as far as readers are concerned.

R: Such as?

JMS: For one thing, transcripts take up far more space than the anecdotal or case history form. Much of it is wasted, blank space.

R: What else?

JMS: They lack the dramatic impact of a well-rounded anecdote, which presents an individual's personal problems and triumphs.

R: Is that all?

JMS: Their wordiness and length can make it difficult for the reader to discern the key point they are supposed to be learning.

Notice the difference it makes when you restate the above in paragraph form: Transcripts have a couple of shortcomings as far as readers are concerned. For one thing, transcripts take up far more space than the anecdotal or case history form – much of it wasted, blank paper. They lack the dramatic impact of a well-rounded anecdote, which presents an individual's personal problems and triumphs. In addition, the wordiness and length of transcripts can make it difficult for readers to discern the key points they are supposed to be learning.

The anecdotal format, on the other hand, creates greater reader involvement by presenting a portrait of someone like the reader, with a similar problem, and then shows how they solved – or failed to solve – their problem. The case history or anecdotal approach is appealing because it is both more dramatic and easier for readers to connect to. Readers prefer them over transcripts every time.

Consider reformatting transcripts into developed anecdotes. Be sure to use all the key elements that go into the making of a good case history (see Mistake #55).

MISTAKE #56
Not Making the People in Your Case Histories Come Alive

When you illustrate your point with an anecdote involving a real-life person (or a composite), you want the story to have emotional impact. You want the reader to see some aspect of themselves in that person. In short, you want the reader to identify with them.

You can't create that sense of rapport by just giving the person's name and then launching into a description of their problem. That leaves the subject of your case history as a nonentity – a faceless stranger with whom the reader cannot really identify. If readers don't identify with them, they don't care what happens next. For example, "Joseph was dyslexic. I tested him and..."

Even if you must change some of the details to conceal your subject's identity, take a couple of phrases or even sentences to characterize him or her for the reader. Give the person's age, describe their job, background, appearance, mannerisms. This will make the person "come alive" for readers and establish the sense of connection you want between them. Observe how Joseph in the example above takes tangible form, and better illustrates the point when you write, "Joseph was a charming, well-bred, highly intelligent young man of 28. Yet, he was shabbily dressed, lived in a rundown apartment, had never graduated from high school or held a job above night-watchman. He was dyslexic. I tested him..."

PART SEVEN
OTHER CRITICAL MISTAKES

Here are nine more errors that can sabotage your book – both during the submission process and after publication.

MISTAKE #57
Failure to Fully Develop Important Ideas and Concepts

You can't just mention a new or linchpin idea and expect the reader to immediately accept it or understand its implications. They won't. You need to take the time to explain the idea, and show why it is valid. Illustrate your points with concrete everyday examples.

Here's a general rule of thumb: The more important an idea, the more space you should spend elaborating on it. Don't use only one sentence to describe something important, and write several paragraphs on a side issue. Otherwise, the reader is going to come away remembering the side issue, not the salient point. On the other hand, if you lavish several pages with illustrations, examples and discussions of your primary topic, you can rest assured you have done all that you can to impress the main point upon a reader's memory.

Let's assume you are writing a book on the "Inner Game" of golf. You can't just say in a sentence, or even a paragraph, that everyone – including the reader – has an "inner golfer" with an innate ability to play golf well, and then go straight on to writing about the things that block us off from this innate ability to play well. If you do, you can count on losing your reader in the process.

For many beginning and experienced golfers, the fact that they have an innate ability to play well will come as a revelation. This new idea will probably feel counterintuitive and may well contradict their own experience on the golf course.

To make a convincing, well-illustrated case to these skeptical readers will take more than a paragraph or two. Most writers discover several pages are required before they are through fully explaining an important point. Pretend again that you're in that situation where you meet someone at a party who, though bright, is a novice as far as your subject is concerned. You want to spell out the central points of your argument in as much detail as necessary for your audience to understand you.

MISTAKE #58
Not Supplying Concrete Examples

This is another authorial lapse caused by knowing a subject too well. You think you have made a point or idea sufficiently clear because you know how it manifests in people's lives. But readers may not have had the experiences to help them make that connection for themselves. They may need some concrete examples to be able to picture how your ideas would play out in real life.

For instance, say you are writing a book about how women can attract a man who is "genuine husband material." You might caution the reader that to attract such a man, women should "reject choices that will cause men to perceive them as unsuitable wife material." To an expert in relationships who has watched women make the same self-sabotaging decisions over and over, it may seem as if everyone else must know exactly what these "choices" are. But your readers may not have any idea what you're talking about. You will need to spell out the self-sabotaging choices you've seen women make: abusing drugs and/or alcohol, developing a reputation as a tramp, or consistently falling for dangerous men rather than the kind that can offer security, faithfulness and love.

Here's another example: In a book on how readers can get in touch with their own "inner wisdom," an author might write that, "Sometimes people are afraid to tap into the source of wisdom that lies within each of us. They may be afraid they will misunderstand the inner guidance they receive and make a disastrous mistake. Or they might fear the guidance they receive will be spurious and make life worse – instead of better." This may seem concrete enough, but not every reader will have had those fears. They may be unable to visualize what kind of mistake they could make while following inner guidance that could lead to disaster, or how it is possible to receive spurious guidance that could make life worse instead of better.

Or, in a book on recovery from Post-Traumatic Stress Disorder, "PTSD plays an important role in all your interrelations with people." This is a sentence few readers will understand unless it is illustrated with examples of the kind of role PTSD can play in interactions with bosses, coworkers, friends, loved ones, clerks at the mall. You've got to be more specific: "PTSD plays an important role in all your interrelations with people. The emotional deadening described earlier can make developing true intimacy with a spouse or lover a near impossibility. The explosive outbursts of anger could strain relationships with coworkers, or even cost you your job."

That's why it's so very critical to make sure you illustrate every point with concrete examples of what you mean. When you finish writing your book, ask a friend who knows very little about the subject matter of your manuscript to review it for you. Have them mark any places where they feel confused. Often, these are places that would be clearer if illustrated with a concrete example. Hint: Most cases will involve how something works or how someone behaves.

MISTAKE #59
Failing to Double-Check All Facts

Rely solely on your memory while writing a book – and it will betray you every time. This is especially true if you are an expert and the fact being cited is something you have reviewed so many times you know it by heart. Libraries are full of books by scholars who, to their eternal embarrassment, misquoted their source somewhere important in the text. The same is true for authors of books on mathematics, astronomy, Shakespeare, the Bible, biology, biography – you name it.

Why add your book to the list? Imagine what would happen if the first editor or agent you sent it to caught the error. Or if the error slipped past everyone involved in the publishing process, and instead was only caught after publication by discerning readers and influential reviewers. Either way, such a gaffe would throw doubt on the validity of everything else you say in your book.

Before submitting your manuscript, check back over it carefully. Verify all quotations, attributions, dates, names, technical spellings, statistics, numbers and other facts. Especially those you are most certain are right.

MISTAKE #60
Overloading the Book with Too Many Subjects and Goals

Often books fail to sell because their authors have unknowingly given them more than one subject and goal. Too many subjects and goals in one book get in each other's way – it's like trying to ride two horses at the same time while each is dashing in a different direction.

The subject of a book is exactly that – the central topic about which you have decided to write. It might be fitness and exercise, investing in the stock market, or meditation. The book's goal is what you hope to accomplish by writing it (or looked at another way, what you want it to help the reader accomplish). It might be living a longer and healthier life through fitness and exercise, or a low-risk investment strategy that grows portfolios more slowly and safely, or reducing stress through meditation.

Typically with a first book, an author will be bursting with many ideas about their subject which they developed over years, and will be on fire to get them all into their manuscript. For instance, the author of a book designed to help the reader eliminate back pain forever might be eager to:

1. Present her or his system

2. Tell the story of all the years his or her life was crippled by unnecessary back pain before discovering these exercises

3. Paint a portrait of what readers' lives will be like when they are free of pain

4. Speculate on what the world would be like if we were all free from pain

Of course, it is possible to touch on all these topics in one book, but not at equal length or with equal emphasis. Trying to shoehorn all four into a book will prevent any one theme from standing out clearly and blunt the impact each makes on the reader. Instead, knowledgeable writers pick one main subject for a book and subordinate the rest to it.

Similarly, it is best to pick one effect you want your book to have on the reader. For instance, your goal in writing a book on back pain might be to

1. Help chronic sufferers free themselves from back pain

2. Show non-sufferers how to avoid back pain

3. Inform a general readership of all the latest scientific data on back pain

4. Teach people how to become more caring, loving individuals

5. Catch the vision of a better, pain-free world

Again, a single book might be able to achieve any one of those goals. But no one book could encompass them all.

The fact is that readers with back pain don't seek

out a book on back pain to make them better people or to change the world. They buy it because they want their backs to stop hurting. If, in the process of discovering how to prevent back pain, they also become better people as an unintended consequence, they won't complain or demand their money back. But, readers who purchase a book to learn about back pain and find themselves reading about something substantially different will feel like victims of "bait and switch." They rarely finish – and never recommend – such books.

All of this goes back to the way readers purchase books, and the way books are sold by publishers. When most people go to a bookstore, they have a specific title, author, or type of book in mind (i.e., a mystery or a book on back pain). If they are seeking help with a problem, that is their sole focus and they want the title, subtitle and description on the back cover to make as clear as possible how the book focuses on their problem and helps them. If they see other messages or themes included with equal emphasis, it blurs the focus of the book for the reader, and they will put it aside in favor of one that stays right on the track of their concerns. Consequently, the bookstores shelve books in a single, rather inflexible category. The only people going to the health section of a bookstore looking for a work on backache will be in physical pain. People looking for a book on personal change (a small number, most are looking for help with a more specific problem) will go to the psychology/self-help section. A book must be sold in one or the other section. Bookstores won't stock a few copies in both!

Each of the four potential books on back pain cited above has a different market; each calls for a different proportion of elements; and each has to be written in a somewhat different style. The reader of each, their expectations, needs, common backgrounds and problems – and the kinds of examples that will illuminate your points – will be different.

Publishers know each of these four potential books has a different audience. You can certainly convince publishers that there are secondary and tertiary audiences. You can even put on a dust jacket of a book on back pain the single line, "freedom from backache means freedom to be your true self and a realignment of your life for the better." But, you can't convince publishers that readers of one of these books want the material to be 1/3 or 50% about any topic other than back pain.

For example, say you were writing a book called *Depth Writing: A 14-Week Plan for Completing Your Book in Your Spare Time.* You could convince publishers that there is a market for a book on writing that goes deeper than mere how-to instruction and, instead, seeks to connect people up with their inner source of creativity. But you can't convince publishers that even spiritually-minded writers who seek out books with the above title will want to read more about inner creativity than about the nuts-and-bolts of "depth writing" and the steps that will carry them forward to a finished manuscript. And as noted earlier, people who want a book on the transformation of the soul won't be looking in the writing section and won't want to read a book with so much material addressed specifically to writers and their problems.

Whichever section the book is sold in (writing or spirituality), the book jacket and writing inside must focus 80-90% on that subject's audience and their needs and interests. Moreover, what is said on the dust jacket must be a focused representation of the book that a bookstore owner can grasp without saying "where do I put this?" The publisher's sales agent can't tell the store manager that this is a book that will enable someone to write a screenplay, great memos and grow spiritually. Bookstore buyers know that most fledgling writers, for instance, wouldn't buy a book to get their soul going; they want to get their writing going. On the other hand, someone who wants a book on how to get in touch with their true self and improve their life is going to buy a book on that from an expert on the subject.

So you simply, absolutely must decide what the main subject and goal of your book will be – and stay focused on that subject or goal while writing and while pitching your work to publishers.

If, on reviewing your completed manuscript, you find that most of your material focuses on a different subject than you originally intended, then it becomes imperative to change the title and theme of your book to reflect the subject you are *actually* writing about. Be honest with yourself and clarify in your own mind what your key interest and message is. Or else pitch out the majority of what you have written and rewrite the manuscript, staying focused on your original, intended theme.

MISTAKE #61
Failing to Answer Questions Raised in Your Book

Nothing drives readers crazier than having an author raise a question in the text that piques their interest – only to find it isn't explicitly answered anywhere in the book. To be fair, most writers answer most of the questions they raise most of the time. But even one unanswered question is one too many. There is certain to be a reader somewhere who thinks that question is the most important one you raise, and who ends up frustrated and dissatisfied because they can't find the answer. They will probably even scan back and forth through the book for a while, convinced the fault lies with them and that they simply overlooked it, before they realize where the true fault lies.

Hint: Keep a list of every question you raise in the text. Review your manuscript when you have finished it. Be certain you have answered each question directly and explicitly at some point in the text. If not, raising them will mislead readers into expectations you do not fulfill.

MISTAKE #62
Trying to Solve Your Writing Problems on Your Own

Writing a book is no picnic. You are constantly coming up against challenges. You're not sure how to express a tricky concept, or you don't know the best way to present your material, or you're looking for a novel way to capture reader attention, or you wish you could put something across as well as you know a favorite author would. If you are a first-time writer or someone whose expertise lies in another field, you can waste hours, days or weeks, trying to solve these problems on your own – because what you are attempting is to reinvent the wheel, at least when it comes to writing.

Think about it. If you wanted to pitch a curve ball, become a cardiologist, or franchise your family restaurant across the country, would you take the same approach? Would you just start out blindly on your own with no knowledge of the subject and attempt to learn everything you need to know about pitching, medicine or business on your own? If you did, it would take you years of trial-and-error experimentation to learn even a fraction of what successful ballplayers, biologists or business people already know. To become a mathematician, for example, you would have to start out by discovering simple addition for yourself, and then work out division on your own, as well as fractions, algebra, calculus, and so on.

Typically, when we want to learn something, we don't attempt to reinvent the wheel. Instead, we save ourselves time and trouble by learning from others who've done what we're trying to do. In short, we make progress the same way so many have: by standing on the shoulders of giants. Yet, few people think to do this when writing.

You can save yourself wasted time and find the solutions to writing difficulties instantly – by going straight to the experts. When you find yourself at a writing impasse and don't know what to do next or how to write something, don't waste time spinning your wheels. Learn from those who have gone before you. There is no reason why you have to do it all on your own. Other self-help authors have faced – and solved – the same writing challenges you face. Pick up a favorite self-help book and see how the author solved the problem stumping you. Then apply the solution in your own book.

(Note: This is not plagiarism. That is copying someone else's words. Here you are simply applying the solution to a problem. The information presented and the words you use are all yours.)

MISTAKE #63
Relying on Repetition, Redundancy and Pet Phrases

Nothing grates on readers' nerves more than reading the same sentences and phrases over and over and over and... Of course it's necessary to reiterate points and recapitulate ideas mentioned earlier in your book. There's nothing wrong with that. But when you do, make certain that you phrase your point somewhat differently every time.

Otherwise you are likely to unknowingly commit the Three Cardinal Sins of Authorial Laziness. As noted in the heading, these are:

1. Repetition
2. Redundancy
3. Pet words and phrases

Though they may seem the same, each is a distinct sin all its own.

Repetition is repeating the same idea or information *in the same words* at several different points in your manuscript. Of course, there are many times when you need to remind readers of ideas and information you have previously touched on or introduced. But find fresh, new way of saying it. Repeating it in almost exactly the same words is the literary version of the old water torture. After the third time, the reader is willing to do anything not to have to experience it again a fourth.

Redundancy is making a point again that has been made so often the reader becomes sick of it and says, "Okay, I got it already! Let's get on to something new." Unlike repetition, you aren't necessarily repeating yourself word for word. Indeed, you may be saying it in a fresh, new way. Instead, redundancy is reiterating something you have said so often it no longer needs – or bears – reiterating. To do so again is redundant.

Pet words and phrases are habitual ways of putting things that creep into your writing, which can prove equally grating. This is different from repetition because you aren't representing the same idea over and over in the same terms. Instead, you are overusing a word like "instead" (which I used three times in this section). Sports writers often overuse words like "slugger." Movie reviewers may rely too much on "exhilarating," "romp" or "triumph." A professor I knew was overly fond of "On the other hand..." What words and phrases do you overuse when writing?

Naturally, in writing the first draft of something as long as a book, it's easy to fall into repetition, redundancy and the overuse of pet words and phrases. No one can be expected to remember the precise way they worded an idea a hundred pages earlier; or to stop the writing flow dozens of times daily to review every sentence they have already written. Instead, review your manuscript after you finish it. Eliminate repetition, redundancy and pet phrases wherever you find them. Hint: If you write on a computer, the "search" or "find" function on your word processing program can be a big help.

MISTAKE #64
Not Fully Identifying Famous People Mentioned in Your Text

In the course of writing your book, you will probably refer to authorities or famous people at some point in the text. You could do this in passing. For instance, you might be writing a book on golf and mention Jack Nicklaus. Or you might be quoting something someone has said or written, like a passage from Tiger Woods' *How I Play Golf*.

When you do this, it is vitally important that the first time you mention an authority, you devote a few words to identifying the individual involved. You may think the person you mention is so famous that, like Tiger Woods, everyone will know who they are – especially golfers. But what about five years from now, or ten? Will everyone know then? Or what about Jack Nicklaus? The average duffer of today may not know he was the Tiger Woods of his era.

The same is true when citing or mentioning professionals, politicians, movie stars – anyone and everyone. Again, you may think everyone must know who William Jefferson Clinton is – but surveys reveal that most people asked to identify Gerald Ford don't remember he was President. Plus, not everyone who reads your book may be up on popular culture, or even American culture.

Steven King and Steven Segal will only be puzzling to them. And merely referring to someone as Professor Feldman or Janet Jepperson, Ph.D. doesn't give readers much hint of the person's particular area or degree of expertise.

Now, picture how much more illuminating these references become when you add a brief identifying tag. "My good friend, Jack Nicklaus, PGA Player-of-the-Year in 1967 and 1972, and six-time Masters winner..." Or, "Gerald Ford, 38th President of the United States, who assumed the office after the impeachment and resignation of Richard Nixon." Or, "Steven King, the best-selling horror novelist..." Or, "Robert S. Feldman, Ph.D., professor of psychology at the University of Massachusetts and author of *Understanding Psychology*..."

Don't make the mistake of assuming that everyone knows who you're talking about. Like a good host at a party, make sure that every guest – even the most famous – is adequately introduced.

MISTAKE #65
Failure to Coin Exciting Buzzwords that Grab Reader Attention

Readers respond to exciting buzzwords and neologisms. Some titles become buzzwords in themselves – "Chicken Soup for the Soul" and "Don't Sweat the Small Stuff," for example. One psychologist I worked with coined a term for the people you meet in life who help you along the way. She called them "Earth Angels" – after the golden oldies song. Another writer, working on a book about how authors cut themselves off from their inner source of creativity, came up with the term "Connection Busters." In my book, *Double Your Brain Power*, I had mini-exercises I called "Brain Power Doublers." If you can find ways to create brand-new buzzwords in your book, you can almost guarantee readers will use them when talking to friends – and that's the kind of word-of-mouth advertising that makes books bestsellers.

CONCLUSION
THE THREE WORST MISTAKES AFTER PUBLICATION

Most writers think that once their book is published they are home free. They don't realize they can still make critical mistakes after their book is out. Yet those mistakes can do more harm to their career than all the writing mistakes put together.

MISTAKE #66
Blaming the Publisher if Your Book Doesn't Sell

Every author dreams that their book will be an enormous bestseller. When sales fail to realize those dreams, writers wrongly conclude that the publisher is to blame. Typically, authors become frustrated, even enraged, and write scathing letters to their agent, editor and publisher blaming the publisher for not doing enough to promote the book, not spending enough on advertising and/or not printing enough copies. Often these accusations become so bitter and hostile that they breach the relation between author and publisher, and the author has to start all over and find a new publisher for their next book. Worse, the author may develop a reputation as a troublemaker, which will make other publishers reluctant to buy their books.

All this blame is misplaced and the relationship rupture unnecessary, even counterproductive. A moment's thought should suggest that publishers don't invest all the money and effort involved in publishing a book in order to sabotage a book's success. Of course they want each book they publish to become a bestseller, and strive their utmost to make it one. But don't forget, over 50,000 titles are issued in hard and soft cover every year (with tens of thousands more now being issued in e-book form.) That means the odds against your book rising to the top – no matter how hard your publisher works at it – are more than 50,000 to one!

Instead of blaming your publisher when your book fails to live up to your dreams, write them "thank you" notes, expressing your gratitude for all they have done on your – and its – behalf. Rather than wrecking the relationship you have already established with your editor and publisher, this will strengthen it. The publisher will consider you one of those rare, but highly-valued, writers who appreciate their efforts. As a result, they will have only the warmest, fuzziest, most positive feelings about you when it is time to consider your next book project. Not only will the publisher be more likely to make a substantial offer for your new book, they also may be twice as determined to see that it becomes a success as well.

MISTAKE #67
Giving Up on Your Book

The first time isn't always the best time. That's as true when it comes to publishing books as it is when it comes to dating. But, as with dating, if your book's sales don't spark immediately, don't give up hope. Things may catch fire the second or third time around.

Many books fizzled when first released. But the authors believed in their work so strongly that they didn't despair. Instead, they hung in with the book and kept trying to pump life back into it – until they succeeded. For example, *Women Who Love Too Much* sold only 300,000 in hard cover, while the author was certain its potential audience numbered in the millions. Robin Norwood kept politely urging the publisher to do more, and when the book was finally issued in paperback, it sold seven million copies.

Below is a partial listing of methods authors have used to resuscitate books that were seemingly stillborn on publication:

* Taking the book directly to readers by selling it during lectures and workshop appearances
* Seeking a new publisher with greater expertise in the book's subject area to reprint it when it goes out of print
* Finding new ways to distribute it – mail-order, websites, specialty catalogues, etc.
* Getting a movie, documentary or television

program made that is based on the book
  * Selling it to newly emergent electronic media – CD-ROM, e-books, computer games, etc.

While I can't guarantee you the extra effort on your part will always turn your book from an apparent loser into a bona fide winner, I can guarantee that if you don't make the effort, your book will always remain a loser.

MISTAKE #68
Not Writing Another Book

Whether your book is a huge success or a total flop, don't stop there. Write another book. That may seem as if it ought to be obvious advice – but it isn't.

I once went back through *Publisher's Weekly*, the trade magazine of the publishing field, and looked at the ads for authors' first books over a ten-year period. Incredible as it seems, more than half of the first-time authors never wrote another book! I can only guess at why: Perhaps they felt they only had one book in them; perhaps their first book wasn't a success and they decided they didn't have what it takes to be a writer; perhaps they became so involved with their professional or personal life they just couldn't make the time to write.

If you are dubious about producing another book, I can't lay to rest every concern you might have. But, I will say that every time I have sat down and talked with an intelligent person who had written a book or was writing one, I have found their head filled with wonderful ideas that would make excellent books. I am certain the same is true of you. As for a book's failure being a sign that you aren't meant to be a writer – the opposite is probably true. More authors whose first books didn't sell well went on to be successes than vice versa. Steven King's first book, *Carrie*, only sold a few thousand copies when it first came out. It was *Salem's Lot*, his second book, that rose to the top of the bestseller lists. Isaac Asimov wrote over 200 hard cover books that sold in the 5000 to 20,000 copy range – until *Foundation's Edge* became the first to appear on any bestseller list.

There are several reasons why you shouldn't quit with one book – or even five or six – but should always write another book. Among them:

* Each book expands your audience, leading to new sales for previous books and increased sales for each new book

* Each book boosts your writing skills, increasing the likelihood that the next new one will sell better

* Each book helps more people acquire insights that can better their lives, and that's the best of all reasons to keep writing.

APPENDICES

APPENDIX A
ONE CHAPTER AND A PROPOSAL – ALL YOU NEED TO SELL YOUR BOOK

HOW EXPERTS AND PROFESSIONAL WRITERS SELL THEIR BOOKS

Before your self-help/how-to book can become a bestseller with readers, you have to sell it to a publisher. You have a better shot at it when you sell your book the way professional writers do. Professionals don't write books first and then sell them – and you don't have to either.

Instead, you can sell your book first – and then write it. How? By getting a contract from a publisher on the basis of a handful of sample pages – you can actually get them to pay you in advance to do the writing!

Selling your book and then writing it may sound too good to be true. But this is actually standard publishing practice. Professional writers always sell their books this way. Because they have strong "credentials" as established authors, publishers know they will deliver a professionally publishable manuscript and feel safe in contracting and paying for their books in advance.

Simply by being knowledgeable and/or experienced in the subject matter of your self-help/how-to book, you have a credential. As a result, the only thing publishers will require from you is a Sample Chapter and a Proposal (see Part One). All you need to do is dangle them before publishers like bait on a hook, and sit back and await offers.

This method has a number of advantages:

* You put almost zero work (though a good deal of thinking) into your book before you sell it
* You get valuable publishing and editorial insights before you write the bulk of the manuscript
* If publishers don't respond, you can revise your approach – which is easier than revising your whole book – and submit again
* It helps publishers schedule books ahead
* It helps you plan out and pursue the best strategy for writing your book

Almost zero work and saves time. Professional writers like this system, and you will too. Writing a book first has too many pitfalls. If the book fails to sell, the time devoted to its writing – months, perhaps years – is wasted. Or even if it is accepted with revisions, hundreds of pages might have to be rewritten to gain publisher approval.

Publisher input – before writing. Writing a Proposal and Sample Chapter also has other advantages. Sometimes the publisher may like your ideas, but not your approach to writing the book. Obviously, publishers feel more comfortable about suggesting you make basic changes in your book when you've only written a few pages, instead of an entire manuscript. Even when no publisher makes an immediate offer on your book, an intelligent reading of the rejection letters may provide you with valuable clues about how to re-slant or reframe the material so that it will sell on subsequent submissions.

Two chances at success. This system gives you two chances at the brass ring. Publishers are always willing to look at a revised book Proposal. Although few outside the publishing industry know it, many major bestsellers only became bestsellers the second time around. The first time they were submitted, these books were rejected by all the major publishers. But their savvy authors paid careful attention to the critiques they received, and made extensive revisions with them in mind. Naturally, the publishers now found those same books irresistible, because the authors' Proposals had been redesigned to reflect exactly the kind of book the publisher wanted.

Helps publishers plan publishing schedules. Publishers find this system works in their favor, too. It offers them a chance to contribute their suggestions for strengthening your manuscript during its formative stages. It also allows them to plan what books they will be publishing over the next few years.

Meanwhile, the six months or a year you spend writing your book after the publisher has contracted it will give its staff sufficient time to develop effective marketing and promotion plans. Those plans must be in place three to six months prior to publication. That is the lead time needed for the publisher's marketing division to sell your book to stores, as well as for print and electronic media to schedule reviews of it and interviews with you.

Helps you plan the best strategy for writing your book. Writing a Proposal for your book has a final advantage. It gives you the opportunity, and framework, for focusing in depth on almost every element of your book before you actually start writing the book itself. In creating the major parts of a Proposal, you will learn how to:

* Precisely define your theme and audience
* Create a "bestseller title"
* Give your book irresistible reader (and sales) appeal
* Develop a bestselling style
* Find the best structure for your book, and the individual chapters and subsections
* Present yourself as an expert whom publishers and the media will clamor to present

WHY YOUR EXPERTISE WEIGHS HEAVILY WITH PUBLISHERS

Publishers are always actively looking for self-help and how-to books written by those with expertise. Publishers know that the vast audience that watches television talk shows – and can make a book a bestseller – is far more impressed when a book is written by someone with special "inside knowledge" of a subject. Talk show producers know it too. That's why they are far more likely to book a doctor, athlete, craftsperson, recovering alcoholic or artist than a journalist who has merely researched a subject and knows about it only second-hand.

What qualifies as an expertise credential to a publisher? Almost any involvement with a self-help or how-to subject area that gives you unique insights and knowledge worth sharing. Publishers, journalists, producers, talk show hosts, readers, and audiences consider you an expert *if you fit one or more* of the following categories:

* Are a professional
* Have received a degree of any kind in your or a closely allied area
* Have practical, hands-on experience in it
* Possess a vital skill that few others have (cabinet making, recovery from addiction, improving your tennis score, repairing plumbing, building a billion-dollar-per-year business, breaking the glass ceiling for women, making marriage work, painting large-scale murals, etc.)

* Have edited publications on or specialized in writing about the subject of your manuscript
* Bring any other form of special knowledge or insight that can be applied to it

If you – or the person you are collaborating with – meet any of the above qualifications (and if you are thinking of writing a self-help or how-to book, you probably do), then publishers will consider you to have expertise in your field. (If you do not feel you have sufficiently strong expertise, you can always consider contacting someone who does, and asking them to become your co-author.) As someone with expertise, or a co-author with an expert, publishers will be eager to read your Proposal, and eager to add you to their roster of authors. More importantly, they will be willing to evaluate and purchase your book before you write it – based solely on a writing sample and short Proposal.

APPENDIX B
THE SELF-HELP WRITER'S MANUSCRIPT REVIEW CHECKLIST

When you finish your book, use this checklist to review your manuscript for key mistakes – before you submit it to agents or publishers. Clear your mind as much as possible and attempt to read the manuscript with fresh eyes – as if you had never seen it before. Scrutinize it for the following:

CASE HISTORIES AND ANECDOTES. Have you introduced them all and characterized each person involved?

CHAPTER THEME. Is the theme of each chapter, as well as how it relates to the overall theme of your book, clear?

CONDENSING. Is there anyplace where the manuscript seems to go on about one subject too long and might benefit from condensation?

DEFINITIONS. Have you defined every technical, academic or professional term? Hint: Look for any words the reader might not find familiar.

EXERCISES. Have you introduced each fully, explained how to do it in sufficient detail, explained how to interpret their results or what changes the reader should expect in their life?

EXAMPLES. Is there any place where you feel the idea being discussed would benefit from being illustrated by an example?

EXPLANATIONS. Are there any important, technical or complicated ideas or concepts that you haven't fully explained?

FACTS. Have you double-checked all dates, heights, populations, statistics, attributions and other facts? Hint: When you trust your memory – it's always wrong.

FLACCID WRITING. Are there places where you have become too wordy? Remember, if you can use one word instead of three, you probably should.

FOCUS. Have you stuck to the main topic throughout a chapter or section? Hint: Look for spots where you have gone on tangents.

HEADINGS AND SUBHEADINGS. Are they plentiful? Hint: You should have one for each new idea or subject.

INTRODUCTIONS. Have you introduced chapters, sections and subsections fully before discussing them?

NEGATIVE COMPARISONS. Have you inadvertently explained only what something is not? Hint: Anytime you discover you have defined something by what it isn't, look back to see if you first remembered to explain what it is.

PROPORTION. Have you given more space to important issues and briefer treatment to less important ones?

QUESTIONS. At some point, have you answered every question you formally ask in the text?

READER INVOLVEMENT. Have you consistently remembered to write the reader into the book? Hint: Is the reader addressed frequently enough through the use of "you"?

RUN-ON-SENTENCES. Do you have any sentences of three lines or longer? Hint: If you can rewrite it into two sentences, you probably should.

RECOMMENDED READING

Print Books

How to Get Your E-Book Published. Richard Curtis. Writers Digest Books 2001.

Negotiating a Book Contract: A Guide for Authors, Agents and Lawyers. Mark L. Levine. Moyer Bell Ltd. 1988.

Publishing Success: How to Create and Profitably Sell Your Writing on the Internet. James Dillehay. Warm Snow Publishing 2001.

The Literary Agent's Guide to Getting Published And Making Money from Your Writing. Bill Adler. Claren Books 2000.

This Business of Publishing: An Insider's View of Current Trends and Tactics. Richard Curtis. Allworth Press 1998.

Writeriffic: Creativity Training For Writers. Eva Shaw. Writeriffic Publishing Group 2001.

Writing the Nonfiction Book. Eva Shaw. Rodgers & Nelsen Publishing Co. 1999.

eBooks

Electronic Publishing: The Definitive Guide. Karen S. Wiesner. Avid Press (annual editions).

Buzz Your Book. M. J. Rose. Pigeonhole Press 2001.

ABOUT THE AUTHOR

Jean Marie Stine has devoted much of her life to researching, teaching, and writing about human potential, especially the optimization of mental performance. First as an editor of psychology and self-help books, then as creator of highly successful seminars on brain power, speed learning, and self-help writing. As an editor, she has worked with many of the leading human-potential and peak-performance consultants, including Jean Houston, Ken Wilber, Charles Garfield, Betty Edwards, Timothy Leary, Marianne Williams, Marilyn Ferguson, and Neil Fiore. She is the author or coauthor of more than two dozen nonfiction books, including *Double Your Brain Power* (Prentice-Hall, 1997), a selection of the Quality Paperback Bookclub and the One Spirit Bookclub; *It's All in Your Head: Amazing Facts About the Human Mind* (Macmillan, 1994); *Writing Successful Self-Help/How-To Books* (Wiley, 1996); and *Unlock Your Hidden Genius* (A&T Books 2014).

Printed in Germany
by Amazon Distribution
GmbH, Leipzig